How to
Give Your Child an
Excellent Public
School Education

■ ■ ■

How to
Give Your Child an
Excellent Public
School Education

■ ■ ■

Susan Mansell

A CITADEL PRESS BOOK
Published by Carol Publishing Group

A Citadel Press Book
Published by Carol Publishing Group
Citadel Press is a registered trademark of Carol Communications, Inc.

Editorial, sales and distribution, rights and permissions inquiries should be addressed to Carol Publishing Group, 120 Enterprise Avenue, Secaucus, N.J. 07094.

In Canada: Canadian Manda Group, One Atlantic Avenue, Suite 105, Toronto, Ontario M6K 3E7

Carol Publishing Group books may be purchased in bulk at special discounts for sales promotion, fund-raising, or educational purposes. Special editions can be created to specifications. For details, contact Special Sales Department, Carol Publishing Group, 120 Enterprise Avenue, Secaucus, N.J. 07094.

Manufactured in the United States of America

10   9   8   7   6   5   4   3   2   1

Library of Congress Cataloging-in-Publication Data

Mansell, Susan.
    How to give your child an excellent public school education / Susan Mansell.
        p.   cm.
    "A Citadel Press book."
    Includes bibliographical references and index.
    ISBN 0–8065–1999–1 (pbk.)
    1. Public schools—United States.   2. Education—Parent participation—United States.   3. School improvement programs—United States.   4. Educational change—United States.   I. Title.
LA217.2.M36   1998
371.01′0973—dc21
                                                98–39567
                                                    CIP

To Francis Louise Pinkerton Mansell (known to everyone as Pinkie) for being the optimistic, cheerful, positive role model that she has always been, and for her constant love and support. Ninety and still going strong.

Thanks to Florence, Dan, Richard, and Alice for the countless hours they spent editing and listening to me. Thanks to Richard for not demanding a divorce during the long process of writing this book. Thanks to Ali and JJ for being proud of me. Thanks to Jane Mushabac, Hui Chen Lu, Steve O'Connor, Gareth Ezersky, Godwyn Morris, Jean Schmidt, Kim Kaufman, Lisa Nord, Clara Hemphill, Shelly, Marge Hudson, Heidi Kaner, Basia Hellwig, Vera Selig, Clare Hammerle, David Levin, Atina Grossman, Clare Mansell, Sue Perry, Bobbie Beck, Tessa Harvey, Carol Shookoff, Sarah Scrymser, Alan Kaufman, Kathy Kline, Daina Shobrys, Susan Simmonds, Helen Santiago, Margaret Johnson, Barbara Shostal, and my editor, Monica Harris.

Finally, a huge thanks to all of the parents and principals from the seven schools in the book. Everyone was so willing to share ideas and enthusiasm for this project. They all deserve credit.

CONTENTS

HOW TO
GIVE YOUR CHILD AN
EXCELLENT PUBLIC
SCHOOL EDUCATION

Children are the world's most valuable resources. As parents, we make a difference in our children's lives not only at home but also, and perhaps more importantly, in their schools. Good teachers and administrators understand that we can make invaluable contributions to our children's schools—contributions that benefit many children, not just our own.

—Pauline Brookfield, parent

Introduction

A revolution in education is going on all over America. Parents are becoming more involved and are exerting their influence on how their children are being schooled. A wide range of options now exists: private school, home schooling, parochial school, public school—even groups of parents starting their own charter schools.

Parents are becoming more involved for many reasons: frustration with the quality of education in public schools; larger classes, fewer supplies, and more cutbacks in enrichment offerings. Parents who might have been happy with the public schools twenty years ago are now looking for other options for their children.

I would like to offer parents some advice: Don't be afraid of the public schools. You may have perfectly valid reasons for sending your children to private school, but those reasons don't have to include the quality of education. Class size is larger in public school, but usually the children work in smaller groups. There are also wonderful advantages to sending your children to public school. Public school is an excellent place for children to learn to get along with children who may be different from themselves. It does not serve our children well to shelter them from others of different races or socioeconomic circumstances. Learning to live together and get along with others in a multicultural environment is an education in itself.

After enrolling your child in school, get in there and try new ideas to enrich your children's education. There has never been a better time to become involved. Schools want parents to help. A mandate called the Compact for Learning in New York State, and similar mandates in other states around the country, gives parents a decision-making role in school management councils, along with the teachers and the principal.

The principal is one of the most important factors in a successful school. A principal who is not only available to parents, but can work with parent groups, not against them, is invaluable. Educating our children is a team effort: principal, teachers, parents, and children—all working together.

When my husband and I began the search for a school for our older child, we had her intelligence tested as a first step. As her IQ scores were very high, we knew we needed to choose a challenging environment for her. The tester was horrified that we might not put her in a private school or a public school for the gifted and talented, where the grouping is homogeneous. We both felt that she would learn more in a heterogeneous grouping in a neighborhood school, where the children have a variety of strengths and talents.

What do these IQ test scores really mean about future success, anyway? In elementary school, children need a nurturing environment to build a strong sense of self-esteem. They need to have successes early in life in order to be able to withstand the later challenges of middle school, high school, and college, not to mention adult life. I wanted her to be excited about learning, not stressed out from competition with other children. We have all heard of children who do not perform well in overly competitive situations in elementary schools.

We chose PS 75 for some specific reasons: First, it was our neighborhood school (two blocks away); second, I liked the principal (an active parent at her own children's neighborhood school); third, our neighbor's son (who is also very bright) went to the school and did very well; and fourth, we knew there were other bright children entering kindergarten with her to serve as a peer group. It was important to me that she had a peer group to keep challenging her to learn more, not merely to coast along as the smartest kid in class.

The school was very ethnically diverse, reflecting our Manhattan, Upper West Side neighborhood. The principal offered no special promises, but she seemed very open to parents' ideas. She was fond of saying that all children are gifted and talented.

My instincts were to give it a try, get involved, and hope for the best. I already knew a number of energetic parents whose children were also entering kindergarten and were willing to work to improve the school. I decided if it weren't challenging enough for my daughter academically, we could always change our minds and enroll her in a gifted-and-talented program or in some other school out of the neighborhood after a year or two.

I had also heard about the active PTA at PS 75, which had "encouraged" the old principal to retire and hired a new one. This sounded like the perfect place for my daughter and for an activist parent like me. At the time I didn't know I was an activist parent. I had loved my elementary school when I was a child and I wanted my children to love their school, too.

I grew up in a small Georgia town with only one school, but it was a good school with a strong music program. My mother was also a positive influence, having been the school nurse as well as the public health nurse for the entire town.

Our daughter has now graduated from PS 75 and our son is in fourth grade at the same school. My daughter received an excellent elementary education and made many good friends. She now attends a public, neighborhood, advanced-program middle school. When my son needed additional services in the early grades for speech and counseling, the school was very supportive of him and now he is thriving.

It has been very exciting for me and the other parents at PS 75 to be part of the process of creating new programs and implementing ideas at the school. The parents at our school have the reputation of being active, caring, and fair-minded. Being involved is very fulfilling for parents who want to make a difference in their children's and other children's education. The school has a spirit all its own. It has become a very popular school with middle-class families in the area.

Now PS 75 is not picture-perfect; many stresses are involved in a diverse racial, ethnic, and socioeconomic population like the one at our school. It is a daily education in human relations. When problems come up, we have the fun of trying to solve them. Parents, principal, and teachers work together as part of the process. More often than not, we are successful in finding solutions.

My children know how important their school is to their parents; they often see me working at the school. I know all their teachers personally, and the kids know they can't get away with anything. The most important thing to me is not policing my children's behavior however, but that both my daughter and son love going to school and ultimately become lifelong learners, continuing to absorb life's lessons, both as students and as adults.

Many other parents like my husband and me are out there, actively supporting their kids' school. We certainly don't have exclusive rights to parent involvement, as you will see from reading about the other schools in this book. The goal of this book is to share ideas and successes from many schools with other parents.

I have interviewed principals, parents, teachers, and PTA presidents in six other schools across the United States. Each school is different, but each one is functioning well because of cooperation among the parents, principals, and teachers.

I have included a short list of helpful websites for parents and some healthy ones for kids. Some of these sites will bring discussion groups into your E-mailbox. This is a good way to use the computer to share ideas with other parents. As a matter of fact, if you have any ideas you'd like to share, please E-mail me at kaufmnsl@sprynet.com.

Family Fun magazine ran a feature article in the September 1996 issue called "The Rebirth of P.S. 75." The article was written by Deborah Weisgall, a professional writer and a public-school parent in Lincoln, Massachusetts. Deborah was so inspired by our urban school that she began meeting with her principal and organizing some projects at her child's suburban school, using some of the ideas from PS 75 as a model. On the surface, the two schools could not be more different. This example shows how children can benefit from the hands-on model of parents, principals, and teachers working together and sharing information with others.

A BRIEF HISTORY OF PUBLIC SCHOOL 75

To get some perspective on why PS 75 is a good example of success, let's look briefly at the history of the school. Public School 75, also known as the Emily Dickinson School, is an elementary school on the Upper West Side of Manhattan in New York City. The school's local neighborhood is ethnically and economically diverse. PS 75 was built in 1950 and for many years was considered a model in its school district for excellent education. Many innovative ideas, including the open classroom and team teaching, originated in the school. Families moved into the neighborhood specifically so they could send their children to PS 75. The school was always well-known in the district for functioning on a very high level. It provided a challenging learning environment for all who attended during those years.

By the mid-eighties, however, the school had changed drastically. It had lost many middle-class parents. The school population had shifted from an economically and racially integrated one to one made up almost completely of economically disadvantaged Latinos and African-Americans, with 78 percent qualifying for the federal free lunch program. Reading scores on the city wide tests had dropped by at least 25 percent.

What happened? The principal who had been so brilliant for the first fifteen years of his tenure had lost his ability to run the school. He was disrespectful to teachers and parents in front of children. His behavior became increasingly erratic. As a result, teachers would close their doors and try to avoid confrontations with the principal. Many of the school's best teachers transferred to other schools. Classrooms were empty due to underenrollment.

In 1989 the Parents' Association decided the time had come to save PS 75. They documented incidents of inappropriate behavior on the part of the principal. They filed a lawsuit citing infringement of their right to free speech when the principal refused to allow the parents to distribute meeting notices on school grounds. They sought help from the district superintendent who, fortunately, supported their position. In a dramatic demonstration, 150 parents showed up at the school board meeting, demanding his ouster. The school board began pressuring him to resign. Ultimately, he retired.

The parents had won the battle, but now the long process of rebuilding the school had to begin. The assistant principal, who was running the school, and the newly formed School Senate, made up of teachers and parents, held a two-day retreat in an attempt to heal wounds and open a dialogue. They discussed many issues, including school structure, curriculum, and what kind of principal they would like to hire for the school. The parents reviewed more than sixty résumés and considered eighteen as serious candidates. The candidate they were most excited about impressed them as a team player. During the interview, the selection committee asked her what accomplishments she was proudest of in her career. Her response was, "Let me say that I have not accomplished anything by myself." According to Laura Friedman, the co-president of the Parents' Association at that time, that was it: She must have been able to work with people to make that statement. In addition to her professional experience as a teacher and administrator, she had been a very active parent in her own children's elementary school in Brooklyn. This was clearly someone who could relate to parents, teachers, and staff. She was chosen for the job.

Roberta Kirshbaum became principal in December 1989. She immediately took steps to improve communication among the staff and encouraged teachers to form groups to discuss reading, writing, math, and other subjects.

As principal of PS 75 for six years, Kirshbaum showed that she was very adept at collaborating with parents and teachers. As a principal, she was really a dream come true for parents. Parents were able to participate fully and work as partners in the education of their children.

In March 1997 PS 75 welcomed another new principal, Robert O'Brien, who replaced Kirshbaum after she had decided to move to another job closer to her home. He was chosen out of a group of over one hundred candidates. He is energetic, fair-minded, and proud to be the principal of the Emily Dickinson School. The parents and teachers are all confident that he will carry the school forward to new levels of excellence. The school that is like a "Little United Nations" continues to be an inspiration to all.

1
■ ■ ■

Parent Power

Power is influence. Because they are the single most important influence in their children's development, parents can use their power in many ways to give them a strong start in life.

Parents are the ones who first encourage their children to love learning—they are their children's first teacher. Children who are read to and taken to the library by their parents are more likely to love books. Children whose parents answer their constant why? why? why? questions will continue to be curious about how the world works long after they can find out the answers for themselves.

That influence continues when the child starts elementary school. Parents give messages about school by their attitude toward it, and children take their cues about the importance of school from their parents. Today's parents can be involved in their children's education in a variety of ways, from helping their individual child with homework to being a member of the school board.

HOW TO HELP YOUR ELEMENTARY
SCHOOL CHILD LEARN

Let's start first with how you can help your own child. After making sure that your child is healthy and well fed, you want to encourage and nurture your child so that learning to read and write is a joy. In the best of all possible worlds, your child will become a lifelong learner.

CLASSROOM TEACHERS

Any parent will tell you that the classroom teacher is the most important person in their child's school experience. The teacher is with your child every day, doing his or her best to inspire them to learn. Most teachers want to establish a home/school partnership to reinforce their efforts with the children. Make sure you have made the effort necessary to develop a working relationship with your child's teacher.

IDEAS TO HELP YOUR KIDS
SUCCEED IN SCHOOL

- Start the school year off right by establishing a good working relationship with your child's teacher. Express your intention to support the teacher at home and at school.
- Write notes to the teacher, call, stop by on your lunch break, or on the way to work to keep up with your child's progress.
- Never miss a parent-teacher conference, which is an opportunity to develop cooperative strategies with the teacher for educating your child.
- Get feedback from the teacher as often as possible.
- Ask questions and express your concerns in a constructive way.

- Ask the teacher how you can reinforce what he or she does in class with your child at home. If your child is having problems in specific areas, ask for advice on how you can "partner" with the teacher to do extra work or give special encouragement that will help your child overcome the problem.
- Volunteer to help the teacher in or out of the class with classroom projects.
- Send your child to the teacher rested, well fed, and ready to learn.
- Show your curiosity about what your child is learning by asking them specific questions about school. Some children don't respond with much detail to parental inquiries, but they will get the message that school is important to you.
- Establish regular times for homework and provide a quiet area for study without interruptions. The child's school materials should be within easy reach. Each child learns differently and the regular study area should be comfortable for your child.
- Check your child's homework for completion. Many teachers in fourth grade and above do not want you to correct your child's work because they want to know how much the child understands without help from an adult. Ask the teacher for the proper procedure. Use homework lists, charts, or notebooks to check off when assignments are completed. Let the child know that completing a task is important.
- If it is approved by the teacher, support your child when he works on school projects. One way to support him is to encourage planning and completing long projects in stages. Mark due dates on the family calendar.
- Take pride in your child's work. Display drawings, poems, projects, art works, and other items in your home in a prominent place.
- Read aloud to your child regularly. And don't stop reading aloud to your child even as he or she gets older. They still like this kind of interaction with a parent.
- Form a reading group with other parents and children to read and discuss favorite books on a regular basis.

- Do not let any negative feelings you may have had about school prevent you from helping your children. Show them that learning is important to you by being a good example.
- Visit the library often. Keep the TV turned off.
- Go to museums, historic sites, art galleries, nature centers, and other cultural and environmental centers.
- Encourage cooperative learning groups informally among your child's friends, sharing information on common interests.
- Encourage your child to keep a journal, to write poetry and original stories, and to write letters to famous people and elected representatives.
- Use the Internet and fun educational software programs to spark your child's curiosity. Puzzle programs and treasure hunts frequently use basic math and memory games.
- Have your child study music, dance, or art in addition to what's offered at school, which can improve their concentration skills and self-esteem.
- Have your child sign up for a sports team in the neighborhood, or start one. Swimming, skating, baseball, soccer, basketball, tennis, and hockey all build strong bodies, teach cooperation, and pride of achievement.
- Have your child join the Boy or Girl Scouts or a similar organization to build character.

PARENTS CAN IMPROVE THE
SCHOOL FOR ALL CHILDREN

In my children's elementary school parents contribute enormous amounts of time and energy for the children. They are so committed to the school that they were the inspiration for this book. Our school has been improved by ideas from parents of children at the school and by ideas from parents in other schools. This spirit of sharing ideas among parents for the good of *all* children is the focus of this book.

The list of things parents can do at their local school is enormous. Let's start by visiting seven public elementary schools to see what their parents are doing to help. Each of these schools, located in a different region of the country, was chosen for its success in educating children. Each of these schools has a different ethnic and socioeconomic population. The seven are urban, rural, and surburban schools; one is a school for gifted students. The common feature for all these schools is active parents.

PS 75, THE EMILY DICKINSON SCHOOL
New York City
Students: 700   Teachers: 50   Grades: K–5
Built in 1950
PTA: 500 (Every parent is automatically a member.)
Principal: Robert O'Brien

PS 75 is known in its Manhattan neighborhood as a school with an unusually active group of parents. The student body includes a wide range of socioeconomic levels with both middle-class and low-income families in the school, reflecting the mixed character of the neighborhood. The federal free lunch program for low-income families has 65 percent participation. A student population of one-third African-American, one-third Hispanic, and one-third Caucasian or other background creates an unusual multicultural climate among students and parents.

Parents volunteer as reading tutors, chaperones on class trips, library helpers, assistants to teachers on class projects, after-school program administrators, new playground designers, translators, and as members of the technology committee, antibias committee, and school planning council.

The building is colorful inside and out, having been decorated by student and professional artists using the interior and exterior doors as canvases. The walls outside the classrooms are covered with children's writing projects and artwork.

On the north side of the building, inset from the sidewalk, is the

Emily Dickinson Reading Garden, a quiet reading spot with benches purchased by parents. The garden was designed and planted by a neighbor who lives across the street from the school. He continues to volunteer his time and money to maintain the garden so children from the school can enjoy it.

The PTA sponsors many social activities for families, such as: an annual square dance, a salsa dance, classroom cleanup day, international night, an auction, a spring carnival, picnics, Black History Month with tours of Harlem, family technology night, and family science night. Some, but not all, of the events combine fund-raising with social activities. The PTA also publishes a school directory every year, which is free to all families. A monthly PTA newsletter, in both English and Spanish, publishes announcements and news of interest to the entire school community.

This school is known as a progressive, idealistic, and very realistic place. Children of university professors go to school alongside children of recent immigrants, some of whom are on public assistance. The educational philosophy involves placing children in heterogeneous classrooms. A K–5 dual language program in Spanish and English has been in place for many years. A respected special education program and resource room serve the community well. Kindergarten, first- and second-grade classes are organized into learning centers that make the large classes seem smaller. Children work in heterogeneous learning groups. The new principal has instituted reading ability groups across the grade for a double period every morning in fourth and fifth grades.

Special programs include offerings in music, art, science, and the computer lab. Teachers and Writers—a program using writing teachers from Columbia University, and paid for by the PTA and the district office—has been at the school for more than twenty years. The parents also pay for band instrument instruction in the fourth and fifth grades.

Teachers take advantage of the school's location in New York City by visiting museums, historic places, and cultural institutions.

Younger children participate in the Little Orchestra Society concert series at Lincoln Center; the older children take part in the Carnegie Hall concert series. Students visit the United Nations and Ellis Island in third grade to complete their study of immigration. There is a full-time music teacher for the kindergarten through second graders and recorder classes for third graders at a nearby music school.

PS 75 has the feel of a small, friendly town. Parents run an after-school program they developed themselves for the school and for the neighborhood children. After-school care is free to fifty children on the free lunch program, for four days a week. Enrichment classes, paid for by parents, include ceramics, sports, computers, karate, and science. The money from these classes helps to underwrite the free after-school care.

The PTA uses Emily Dickinson's name to encourage children to love poetry and literature. Colorful T-shirts with her poetry are for sale in the school store, called Emily's Bookstore. The store, run by teachers and parents, is located outside the lobby.

Once a year Dee Ratterree, the energetic, full-time parent volunteer who runs the school library committee, puts up a leafless reading tree made of construction paper. A leaf is added with the child's name on it whenever he or she finishes reading a book. The children love to point out their names written on the bright green leaves.

Drawings of book characters are sometimes attached to the walls of the school with the message, Pick a Poem from My Pocket. The poems in the pocket are written by students. Emphasis is placed on reading and writing because PS 75 is a magnet school for literature.

The Emily Dickinson School has improved dramatically in recent years through the efforts of parents, principal, and teachers. When the popular principal who started the renaissance at the school left to take another job, the parents rallied around the school. After an extensive screening process by the district office, parents, teachers, and the school board, a new principal was hired. In new principal

Robert O'Brien's capable hands, the school is enjoying stability, steadily rising reading and math test scores, and many innovative programs.

FINDLEY OAKS ELEMENTARY
Duluth, Georgia
Students: 860   Teachers: 50   Grades: K–5
Built in 1993
PTA: 600 members
Principal: Sadie Etris

Findley Oaks Elementary is a recently built school located in a fast-growing suburb of new subdivisions built for corporate employees on the north side of Atlanta, Georgia. The area is growing so fast that the county has to build schools as fast as it can to meet the continuing demand. Most of the families in the school are middle class. A small number of students qualify for the federal free or reduced-price lunch program. The ethnic makeup of the school reflects the community: 88 percent Caucasian, 6 percent Asian-American, 3 percent African-American, 1 percent Hispanic, and 1 percent multi-racial.

The school is named for the Findley family, who owned the land where it was built. The community is so close-knit that, at the dedication of the new school, a member of the Findley family organized a historic reenactment of a Civil War event for the children and their families. Soldiers were dressed in military uniforms riding horses. Women and children wore long period dresses. It was a colorful history lesson for the children and their families.

The PTA is very energetic and contributes significantly to the life of the school. Parents pay $10 for a membership and receive the school directory. The PTA has thirty-seven different committees, including: Public Affairs, Ways and Means, Health and Safety, Environmental Action, Yearbook, Student Support, Academic, Membership, Market Day, Legislative, Family Fun, Volunteers,

Interior Beautification, Recycling, Helping Hands, and Classroom Coordinators.

One very unusual committee is called Dads for PTA, which is specifically run by and for fathers. Chairman Rick Matarrese says that he was inspired to form this committee because he is a single parent and wanted to become more involved in his child's education. He puts out an annual survey of the parents, looking for fathers who might be interested in participating. The stated goal of Dads for PTA is "to increase the involvement of dads in their children's endeavors through participation in all facets of their educational activities via various PTA programs and projects. Our children need to know that dads care too. It is our goal to more greatly encourage dads to participate by providing motivation, opportunity, and example."

The stay-at-home parent, according to Rick, if there is one, has traditionally been the mother. While Dads for PTA was created to involve fathers, in the broadest sense it tries to finds ways to include the working parent, whether that parent is a mom or a dad. For example, Dads for PTA sponsors events like the Breakfast for Working Parents, which is held annually. At this event, parents who cannot come to school to have lunch with their children can visit their child's classroom and feel more connected to the school community.

Dads have been involved in various projects at the school: In one project, dads and their children assembled and delivered a large number of bookshelves and desks, needed for new students, to the appropriate classrooms. Dads have also taken on the monthly grounds maintenance chores that the county has been forced to stop funding.

A group of four dads purchased and installed mailboxes on all classroom doors to cut down on classroom interruptions. The Christmas Tree Recycle was another successful effort by dads along with their children: Over one thousand trees were shredded and the mulch saved for use on the school grounds. Two fathers installed needed shelving in the Lost and Found Room. Some others helped out with the monthly distribution of purchased food products for a fund-raising campaign.

While working dads are very active in PTA committees, working and stay-at-home moms also volunteer at the school. One example of volunteers during school hours is called the Science Force. This national program was started by a group of retired grandparents at another school, who had expertise in the field of science; they later expanded the program. This is how it works: A group of parents conducts hands-on experiments with the students in a special science room. The science kits come from the school, but parents donate their time to help teachers with a learning experience that would be too time-intensive for teachers to set up themselves.

Once a year the PTA sponsors National Drug Awareness Week, pinning symbolic red ribbons on everyone—and to the school building—to call attention to the problems of drug abuse among children. The large ribbon on the school advertises the event to the whole neighborhood. Guest speakers come to the school during the week to talk to children and parents about drug abuse prevention.

The PTA has a Teacher Grant Committee that awards several grants each year to teachers, based on their own proposals. The committee is composed of two teachers and two parents who are not on the PTA Board. The awards range from $50 to $2,400, and have been used to purchase such items as special dictionaries, slow-motion cameras, and music for the choral program. Awards are based on the learning possibilities developed in the teacher's plan. The teachers in the school love this idea, because they are rewarded for their ideas and creativity in a very visible way.

Findley Oaks is a model of parent, principal, and teacher teamwork. It receives a lot of local media attention for its spirit and its new ideas. As a new school with an outstanding principal, it does not carry with it the resistance to change that older schools might have. It is successful not only because it is a new school, but because of the willingness of the adults involved to give their time to the school.

DRY RIDGE ELEMENTARY
Dry Ridge, Kentucky
Students: 582   Teachers: 40   Grades: K–6
Built in 1938, but the school was established in 1868
PTA: 287
Principal: Constance Deats

Dry Ridge is in a rural area near Lexington, Kentucky. This school is recognized on the national level by the U.S. Department of Education as a School of Excellence, becoming a National Blue Ribbon winner in 1997. The Dry Ridge Elementary School Council is a model for school councils around the nation. Dry Ridge Elementary has approximately 49 percent federal free lunch students, meaning that half the student body is at a low-income level. The student population includes a growing number of Spanish immigrants, currently 15 percent to 20 percent of the school.

The school has adopted a policy of inclusion for all special education children, from autistic through children with mild delays. There is a preschool on the premises for developmentally delayed children who are four to five years old. Most of the children in this program have delays in language development. These students remain in the school beyond preschool years. The school provides counseling and follow-up activities with parents whose children are developmentally delayed. Home visits are made to these families by the school counselor, principal, and language teacher, together. They usually arrive at dinnertime and come with a large pizza for everyone to share while they have a meeting.

The school has a wide range of student abilities, from autistic to gifted. In spite of its mixed-ability student population, Dry Ridge receives a large cash scholastic achievement award from the state of Kentucky every award year. The amount of the award is based on the students' high scores on state-wide tests administered every two years in the fourth and fifth grades. The areas covered by the tests include math, writing, reading, science, fine arts, vocational, and social studies. This program is a result of a Kentucky law that attempts to spread state money more equitably to schools in lower-income areas.

The PTA at Dry Ridge encourages parent involvement on any and all levels. Many of the school's families have both parents working full time, so the PTA has to come up with creative ways to involve families in school activities. One such idea is the annual Grandparent's Day. During this day grandparents and other senior members of students' families are invited to a luncheon in their honor at the school. It is always a success, usually with more than eight hundred seniors in attendance.

Another solution is to have parents do school jobs at home, such as covering sets of paperback school books that travel from class to class with clear contact paper, extending their useful life. PTA meetings and back-to-school nights are held from 6:30 P.M. to 8:00 P.M. at night, so that working parents can get home at a reasonable hour during the week.

A PTA coordinator puts together teachers and parent volunteers. The coordinator uses a parent survey asking when, how, and what parents are willing to do for the school. This information is put into a computer database and printed out for teachers. The list is usually posted in the teachers' lounge near the telephones. A parent-teacher resource center is located near the teacher's lounge; books on parenting and other educational books are part of a lending library.

Most parents at Dry Ridge cannot afford to volunteer their time to help in the classrooms without being paid. Those who work with the teachers on a regular basis are paid by the district as instructional assistants. All instructional assistants are interviewed by the school council before being hired.

The PTA also organizes a winter coat drive every year to provide warm clothing for families and children who need them. The local Lion's Club works closely with the school providing used eye glasses for children and parents who cannot afford them.

Every year the PTA sponsors two major fund-raisers: a Fall

Festival and a Santa Shop. The once-a-year Santa Shop is staffed by parents. A list of items available for sale in the shop and their prices is sent home for the children and parents to make their selections. When the shop was first created, many of the items were donated. In more recent years, in order to save time for working parents, 90 percent of the items in the store are purchased wholesale for resale by the PTA. Every gift that goes home is gift wrapped by a parent volunteer. This store saves parents' shopping time, teaches children about money, and is a fun way to make money for the school.

The PTA encourages membership by offering a pizza party to the class or classes with the highest number of participating parents each year. The PTA gives money to the teachers every year if the teachers have a specific plan for spending the money. Items such as VCRs, TVs and other equipment are replaced this way.

One exciting science curriculum project funded by the PTA is a permanent outdoor weather station hooked up to a computer in the building. The information is sent by computer modem to a local TV station, which in turn reports hourly temperature readings from the Dry Ridge Elementary Weather Station. The students can hear the report on their classroom TV, and they understand where and how the TV station got the information.

Dry Ridge's success is due in part to the efforts of its parents. They have come up with a support system that enables all parents to be a part of the school. Active PTA parents eventually find their way onto the school council, where they enjoy making policy for the school. With parents like these and a superb staff, it is no surprise that Dry Ridge is a National Blue Ribbon Winner.

BEVERLY FARMS ELEMENTARY
Potomac, Maryland
Students: 550   Teachers: 24   Grades: K–5
Built in 1965
PTA: 400 family memberships
Principal: Laura Siegelbaum

Beverly Farms Elementary School is a public school that has had an outstanding reputation in its upper middle-class neighborhood for many years. The school is part of the Montgomery County School System in the suburbs of Washington, D.C. The student body is 74 percent Caucasian, 4.2 percent African-American, 15.4 percent Asian-American, 2 percent Native-American, and 5.5 percent Hispanic. A small number of children receive free or reduced-price lunches.

Former PTA copresident Barbara Sherbill describes the role of the PTA as "filling in the gaps that the school doesn't cover to bolster the quality of education for the students." The Beverly Farms PTA has a very committed group of volunteers who spend a lot of time working at the school. For example, the parents help the second-grade teachers by coming to Career Day and talking with the children about their work. This is part of the social studies curriculum on communication. In third grade when the children study Mexico, parents prepare a fiesta luncheon party for students and teachers complete with costumes, music, and a Pinata. In kindergarten through second grade, the parents volunteer to sit at a portable computer, which is wheeled into the hallway, and work with every student on a one-to-one basis. The teacher gives the parent volunteer a checklist of what each child needs to work on. The skills reviewed with the students include math facts, phonics, beginning reading, and simple word processing. The same parent comes to the same classroom once a week for the whole year.

Parents offer after-school clubs for grades one to five, including chess, Little Feet (an aerobics class), and tae kwan do. These classes are open to students for a small activity fee. Hands-on-Science—an outside vendor—trains parents to perform experiments with the kids. Courses vary every year. Parents also run and manage a school store with help from students, selling pencils, paper, notebooks, and a few fun items for kids, including waterbottles, caps, and T-shirts with the school logo.

Every month the PTA publishes a newsletter called the *Eagle*

Express. The newsletter includes a regular column by the principal. The school counselor also writes about topics of interest. They also run reports from teachers and students in every grade. The PTA publishes a phone directory of students and a school calendar for members, which lists the dates when school is in session for only half-days during the year. A family membership in the PTA costs $20.

The PTA is very successful at fund-raising, from activities requiring little effort, to the yearly silent auction in the fall. An example of one of their easy fund-raisers is a pizza party at a local pizza place. The restaurant gives 25 percent of the cash receipts back to the school. Another example is Bingo Night: The PTA sells bingo cards, charges admission of $2, and sells pizza from a local pizza place with 25 percent of receipts going to the school.

Once a year the PTA sponsors a new book fair in the gym. At this event parents volunteer to sell books and other items. This book fair is sponsored by a children's book publisher, usually Scholastic, which delivers the books and picks up the unsold books at the end of the sale, giving the school a percentage of sales.

Every other year the PTA puts on a used-book fair where parents sell donated books. This book fair requires two to three weeks work for the parents to sort and price all the books. The books are put out on tables in the cafeteria for the students to purchase. When the four-day sale is over, Goodwill comes to the school to pick up the unsold books.

In addition to the active parents who help out at school, there is one-in-a-million building services manager, Phillip Baldwin. He does an excellent job keeping the school shining clean and in good repair; but he also does much more. He opens school early to teach basketball to any children who want to learn. Using the name Dr. Phil Good he has been the DJ at the PTA Sock Hop. On Saturdays, when parents hold yard sales, he comes and helps out all day without being paid. He is treasured by children, parents, teachers, and the principal at Beverly Farms.

According to Lynn Klein, the current PTA president, parents want to show their appreciation to all the staff more frequently than the yearly staff appreciation week. In order to do this, the PTA sponsors a monthly event called Something Special. Each month is different. Sometimes they purchase bagels and coffee for everyone. One month each staff member received an individually wrapped brownie with a poem attached to the top. Here is the poem, written by a parent.

> Your energy is boundless
> We thank you for so much.
> In your work with our children
> You have found the magic touch.
> With deep appreciation
> For everything you do,
> The kids at Beverly Farms
> Are so lucky to have you.
> —From the Beverly Farms
> students and families

Beverly Farms is an example of a good school made better by parents who have the time and energy to put into it. This continual support by the parents helps Beverly Farms remain successful.

WESLEY GAINES SCHOOL (named for a World War I hero)
Paramount, California, near Los Angeles
Students: 1,000   Teachers: 49   Grades: K–8
Built in 1953, six original buildings, thirty-eight new trailers
PTA: 200
Principal: Richard Morgan

Wesley Gaines School is a K–8 year-round school that has been the recipient of many awards, including the California Award for Title I Achievment. Title I is a federally funded program for schools with a large percentage of students qualifying for free lunch. Gaines is located in an urban area north of Long Beach, south of Downey and east of the city of Compton. This is a school where 87 percent of the students qualify for the federal free or reduced lunch program. The student body is 70 percent Hispanic, 21 percent African-American, 5 percent Caucasian, 2 percent Pacific Islander, 1 percent Asian, and 1 percent Native-American. The number of limited English-speaking students with Spanish as their primary language is 437, and 246 of these students receive their instruction in Spanish.

The parents at Wesley Gaines School are very involved in the education of their children. Many of these parents are recent immigrants who do not speak English. In spite of this, they work closely with the staff at the school, who make sure that workshops and other parent events are offered in both Spanish and English.

The staff at the school has the following vision for the school: "Wesley Gaines believes that education is a cooperative effort among home, school, and community." To accomplish this, the parents sign Title 1 Parent Compacts, called Partners in Learning; these are yearly written agreements between the parents, the teachers, and the students. Students are being prepared to become responsible citizens and productive members of society, by developing proficiency in reading, writing and mathematics. The school also works to develop "positive character behaviors" such as good work habits, teamwork, perseverance, honesty, self-reliance, and consideration for others. Each day begins with a class leading the entire school community in both the Pledge of Allegiance and in singing a patriotic song. There is a mandatory uniform policy for all students. The PTA holds monthly assemblies to present awards to students. The awards are for good citizenship and for perfect attendance.

Due to the non-English speaking nature of the student body, the school is especially diligent in teaching reading skills to students. In grades K–3 the parents are trained in reading strategies to support their child. One of these programs is called I Have a Parent Who Reads To Me. This program involves 120 kindergarten and first-grade families who check out a big book and video weekly in English or Spanish. WOW! I Can Read! is another program that involves about fifty second-grade families who check out a book weekly in English or Spanish.

Book Bridges is a daily cross-age tutorial program using students on the month-long vacation, which occurs every three months on the new year-round calendar of California schools. These fourth-through eighth-grade students can choose to volunteer two hours every day in the classroom. They tutor students in kindergarten through third grade during school hours in reading the language of their instruction, English or Spanish. Tutors are trained by the Site Literacy Teacher in reading strategies and how to prompt for independent reading. Questions such as "What can you do when you come to a word you don't know?" "Think about what makes sense," or "Did you check the picture?" challenge younger students to become independent readers.

The tutors are given a class set of books that are designed for specific grade levels. After reading a book together in the classroom, the tutor signs the book out to be read at home. The book is placed in an envelope and sent home so the student can read it to a family member that evening. The next day, the book is checked in and a new book is read and signed out to the child. Over two hundred upper-grade students have participated in this daily program since August 1995. The school awards them a special certificate of appreciation and accomplishment at a school assembly when they come back back from vacation. This is a great way for older students to reinforce their own reading skills while gaining self-esteem from teaching younger children. The younger children benefit from the individual attention and encouragement of an older student. Their efforts are reinforced when the child reads the book to a family member.

Parent visitation days are a popular way to keep the parents of Wesley Gaines School aware of what is happening in the classrooms.

Parents meet as a group to discuss what they will see and what they should look for. They observe a teacher-taught lesson in the same subject area. The parents then regroup to openly discuss what they saw. The last step is the evaluation of parents' observations by the staff.

Parents and staff work together to provide a minimum of three parent visitation days a year. The parent involvement group also provides English-as-a-Second-Language (ESL) courses to parents through Adult Education. Yearly parent/teacher conferences are well attended with parents' attendance rates at 98 percent.

Family Nights in reading and math include parents, teachers, and children working side-by-side to learn grade-appropriate concepts and skills. They are held once a year in both Spanish and English. The Family Science Night presents ideas for science projects to parents and children. Materials for projects are described to the parents, and parents get a chance to learn about the scientific process. The entire staff implements this science experience.

Parents volunteer in grades K–3, assisting teachers in the classroom learning centers. These small groups of children working together on different subject areas are part of the balanced literacy program. Centers have subject areas such as writing, math, and reading.

Parents also help out at the Turkey Trot, a celebration of Thanksgiving. Turkey Trot includes food, and presentations of American history as well as foot races for children. Parents serve on the site-based council, which approves funds for the year.

PTA president Stacey Deak listed some fund-raising activities of the PTA, including selling gift wrap, candy, T-shirts, ID bracelets, and nachos at Back-to-School night. Membership in the PTA is $5, which offers discounts on T-shirts and ID bracelets.

The level of parent involvement at this urban school is impressive. The school staff has placed a priority on working together with families to educate the children. Wesley Gaines School is a model for other Title I schools around the country.

KULA ELEMENTARY SCHOOL
Maui, Hawaiian Islands
Students: 500   Teachers: 28   Grades: K–5
Built in 1964
PTA: 200
Principal: Rene Yamafuji, acting principal while regular principal
   Jules Ino is on leave for the year.

This school is on the beautiful island of Maui in Hawaii, in the small community of Kula. Many of the families live in remote areas outside of the town. Kula's student population is diverse: 50 percent Caucasian, 20 percent Asian, 10 percent Hawaiian or part Hawaiian, and 15 percent other. There are 18 percent free lunch, 30 percent upper-income, and 52 percent middle-income families at the school.

   The school has a breakfast program and an after-school program that runs until 5:30 P.M. for latchkey children. Both these programs are run by the staff. An after-school tutoring program is offered at no cost to parents, but there is a limit on the number of children who can be accepted.

   The PTA pays for extra specialists to teach at the school, such as water safety instructors. Even though the children who attend Kula School live on the island of Maui, many do not know how to swim. According to Alan Kaufman, a recent PTA president, this is because many live "up country" in the hills, away from the beaches, and don't have an opportunity to go swimming very often. In addition to swim instruction, the PTA pays for a creative movement teacher to work with two different grade levels, which alternate every year.

   Parents volunteer in such diverse areas of the school as teaching art, driving, and chaperoning. A parent serves as advisor for the student council. Parents help the teachers select software for their class computers. They also work with children on an individual basis, listening to them read aloud to improve their skills. Every class has a "room parent" who facilitates activities for the class, such as field trips.

   Parents volunteer for such after-school projects as the

Thanksgiving Play. This is a play put on by fourth and fifth graders, and directed by a parent who is also a teacher at the school.

Parents help out every year with the annual Halloween Parade, which takes place during school. They work in the spring at Campus Beautification Day, weeding, planting, and painting. Volleyball and football leagues are coached by parent volunteers. Parents help organize the February Fun Run where students get pledges for donations to the school for each minute they run.

The PTA wisely organizes a spaghetti dinner in order to get a large turnout at the first meeting of the school year. They charge a small amount for the food to cover expenses. By providing dinner, they enable more people to come to the meeting.

The PTA pays a parent to coordinate activities and projects with the community. The coordinator quietly makes sure that any child who cannot afford supplies for school will have them.

The annual Harvest Festival raises much of the money for the school and is a social event for all. This festival is described in detail in the chapter on fund-raising.

Kula Elementary School is part of a close-knit small town and rural area. The school has no need for a school directory since everyone already knows everyone else. It is a school that is supported by parents and nonparents alike as an important part of the community.

MANCHESTER ELEMENTARY SCHOOL
Fresno, California
Students: 730   Teachers: 28   Grades: 2–6
Built in 1955
PTA: 350
Principal: Russ Painter

Manchester GATE (Gifted and Talented Education) is part of the Fresno Unified School District, the fourth largest school district in the state. Since it opened in 1955, the building has been home to a variety of schools. Thirteen years ago, Manchester Elementary

School became a magnet school for identified gifted and talented students. Students are admitted to the school based on qualifying test scores. They come from all of the Fresno Schools and are transported by bus. The student population is diverse, which reflects the school district: 49.9 percent Caucasian, 25.6 percent Hispanic, 6.7 percent African-American, 14.7 percent Asian, 1.5 percent American Indian, 1.2 percent Filipino, and 0.3 percent Pacific Islander. Approximately 25 percent of the students qualify for federal free or reduced-price lunch.

In addition to the twenty-three classroom teachers in grades 2 through 6, a science teacher, a computer lab instructor, and a Spanish teacher instruct all students on a weekly basis. Both full-time and part-time music teachers offer instrumental music instruction for all interested students (about 350).

The multipurpose room reflects the warm and friendly atmosphere of the school with displays of student work and acknowledgement of student achievements. The school offers a very wide range of activities and clubs in music, athletics, service, student government, and academic competitions. The list includes: Student Council for grades 3 through 6, Traffic Patrol, Peach Blossom Festival, Computer Club, Tournament of Champions Academic Decathalon, Geography Bee, Talent Show, Manchester Melodies, Mini Melodies, Band, Orchestra, and Odyssey of the Mind.

Intramural sports programs are available to interested students at noontime. School teams that participate in local leagues include: flag football, volleyball, basketball, crosscountry, track and softball.

The entire student body at Manchester participates in community activities. The children perform skits or play musical instruments for patients as part of a neighborhood partnership with Sierra Community Hospital. They participate in ongoing recycling projects. They have designed advertisements for merchants as part of a local newspaper's Design an Ad Contest. The student council participates in neighborhood graffiti Paint Outs that cover over any graffiti-ravaged walls around the neighborhood. Members of the student council volunteer time and services at the Poverello House (a local shelter) and at Valley Children's Hospital. The council sponsors writing contests related to Red Ribbon Day (Drug Abuse Prevention), Arbor Day, and International Peace in Education Day. These activities train the children to be role models, leaders, and active participants in their community.

The students are also involved in history projects. One project in 1994 involved the fifth-grade students in a living history presentation of a colonial village. The children wore period costumes in rooms furnished authentically, going about the daily activities of the colonists. This presentation took place on three evenings so that parents and friends could all have a chance to come.

In honor of the 250th birthday year of Thomas Jefferson, students from Manchester GATE participated in the Jefferson Commemorative Gardens Project. They planted plants from the time of Jefferson in a special historical garden, wrote journals with entries about the experience, and took photos that were sent to the Thomas Jefferson Memorial Foundation in Charlottesville, Virginia.

The Manchester GATE PTA is very active. The executive board of the PTA meets monthly and includes the officers, committee heads, two teachers, and the principal. Three general PTA meetings a year usually include the band, orchestra, or chorus in a performance for the parents. These concerts insure that more parents attend the meetings. The PTA also puts on programs of interest to parents to encourage attendance.

One such program is called Career Night. At this meeting an outside counselor is invited to advise parents about their children's portfolios. Parents whose children want to attend Ivy League schools can find out what kinds of things their children should do to get into gifted middle and high schools. By starting in elementary school, parents and students have time to make intelligent choices that will help on college applications. For example, the middle school and high school gifted programs use grades and portfolios to accept students, not test scores. Extracurricular activities such as volunteer work, sports, and musical activities look good in a portfolio, and the students and parents at Manchester want to be prepared.

Other topics of interest to parents at PTA meetings have included "How to handle a gifted child" and "Why children who study a musical instrument show improved mathematical ability." Refreshments are always served at general meetings. Back-to-School Night includes an ice cream social.

Membership in the PTA is $5, which entitles the member to a school directory, a subscription to the National PTA magazine, and the right to vote on the budget. During the year parents put in requests of what they would like to see included in the budget. An annual vote of members is held to decide how to spend PTA funds for the following year.

According to Nida Palmore, a past PTA president and current school site council member, a wealth of information is included in the Handbook of the National PTA, with information on scholarships for teachers, students, and nurses. Leadership training from the national office is available for parent workshops. The Manchester PTA has taken advantage of many offerings from the handbook. One example is the Reflections Program, a cultural arts program developed by the National PTA.

Many fund-raising events are sponsored by parents. A Mardi Gras celebration in the fall includes a silent auction. A gift wrap sale and a holiday gift shop are run by parents and children. In February a sweetheart raffle is held to celebrate Valentine's Day, giving away prizes like a weekend for two in Monterey. Some of the money from these fund-raising efforts helped build a new playground at the school.

Red Ribbon Week is celebrated by the PTA by inviting community leaders to speak to the children about their jobs in assembly programs. Sportcasters and newscasters from local TV stations, performing artists, and members of the Kiwanis Club have been among the guest speakers.

The PTA also sponsors an annual Multicultural Day with

performances, costumes, and food from different cultures from 5 P.M. to 8 P.M. on a school night. Costumed performances by families have included Japanese drums, Hawaiian dances, and a Nigerian dance.

The PTA gives a staff appreciation luncheon toward the end of the year. They also provide gifts for the entire staff at Christmas. Landscaping is also done on a regular monthly basis by the parents.

The school participates in the Odyssey of the Mind competition, with parents coaching students for district, county, and regional competitions. The students and parents also participate in the Globe Project, using NASA information from the Internet to complete a study of weather and other topics. A parent started the chess club and competition, and a parent coaches the Geography Bee.

Parents helped create web pages for each class. They have donated computers, scanners, and printers to classrooms that need them. Parents have also donated a laminating machine and operate it for teachers as needed for class projects.

Parents chaperone trips to such places as San Francisco, the La Brea Tar Pits, or the county fair. Parents also work with teachers on units like the study of how applesauce is made. From picking apples to cooking and eating the finished product, parents help out every step of the way.

One parent, a professional artist, painted two wall murals in the school. The staff room wall now has colorful flowers and creeping vines. The other mural, in the principal's office, shows a swamp with an alligator in it. The 'gator is the school's symbol.

Because Manchester is a school for gifted and talented students, the children here are offered more activities and programs than are available in most schools. Yet any of its programs could be implemented in regular neighborhood schools when parents, teachers, and principals work together.

TITLE I
PARTNER IN LEARNING
Student – Parent – Teacher – Administrator Agreement

We know that learning can take place when there is a combination of effort, interest, and motivation. As we are all committed to _____'s progress in school, we are going to do our best to promote his/her achievement.

This agreement is our promise to work together. We believe that this agreement can be fulfilled by our team effort. Together we can improve teaching and learning.

As a student I pledge to:
- Discuss with my parents what I am learning in school.
- Adhere to and respect the Student Responsibilities.
- Pay attention and ask questions when I don't understand something.
- Limit my television watching, computer games and read at least 30 minutes a day.

_____
Student Signature

As a parent I pledge to:
- Provide a quiet study time at home and encourage good study habits.
- Discuss with my child about his/her school activities every day.
- Discuss and support the Student Responsibilities.
- Limit my child's television watching and computer game time and ensure that he/she reads at least 30 minutes a day.

_____
Parent Signature

As a teacher I pledge to:
- Provide motivating and interesting learning experience in my classroom.
- Communicate and cooperate with each parent to ensure the best education possible.
- Guide students in their choice of television programs and selection of quality literature.

_____
Teacher Signature

As a principal/facilitator I pledge to:
- Create a welcoming environment for students and parents.
- Ensure a safe and orderly learning environment.
- Reinforce the partnership between parent, student, and staff.
- Provide appropriate inservices and training for teachers and parents.

_____
Administrator Signature

WE PROMISE TO HELP EACH OTHER CARRY OUT THIS AGREEMENT

Signed on this _____ day of _____ 19 _____

2
■ ■ ■

Good Ideas and Instructions

The ideas and instructions for this chapter have been gathered from many sources. Some come from the seven schools profiled in chapter 1; other ideas have been contributed by parents in E-mail chat groups, community websites, and magazine articles. A conference on parent involvement at Teacher's College in New York City was a wellspring of ideas. Networking with friends and educators around the country and extensive reading on education have also been important sources of inspiration.

This section is divided into three different areas: 1. improving the physical plant; 2. raising the academic performance of the students; and 3. improving community spirit inside and outside of the school. Readers can skim this chapter for new and practical ideas. The many helpful hints included from parents' experiences of what actually works in the real world can help guarantee the success of specific projects.

IMPROVE THE PHYSICAL PLANT

Adopt-a-Door

Transform school doors into works of art done by the children. Shelly, the parent creator of this program at PS 75, thinks the process is more important than the end result. "Most kids go to the museum and they see a painting; but I don't think they know how it gets from the tubes of paint to a formal hanging canvas. This process has really shown them. It starts out with an idea, then a design, then color. They learn with teamwork and cooperation that you can finish a project. Ownership gives children more pride in their school. If art can 'wake up' even one kid who finds school boring, then it's worth it."

The first step in painting original murals on school doors is to get approval from the principal. Once this is given, the parent in charge of the project sends out flyers to parents asking if they would like to sponsor a door. Number each door and sell sponsorships for each one for $10 to $20, or more. This provides the money needed for paint, and the people who contribute the money will feel that the door is "theirs."

The next step is finding professional or talented amateur adult artists to volunteer their time, helping to design and paint a school door with the children. Young children need guidance to work effectively together on a project for the whole school. They will benefit from a talented artist showing them possibilities for inspiration, and organizing their creativity. Working with the teacher can also tie the project into the classroom curriculum.

EXAMPLES OF THEMES PAINTED ON SCHOOL DOORS

Stencils of farm animals for kindergarteners
Sponge painting of fruits and vegetables
A collage of students' faces
Underwater scene with fish, octopus, coral reefs, and so on
Night sky constellations

Rainforest animals in their natural habitat
Children's interpretation of a Matisse painting
Map of the earth with flags from many countries represented
Birds, insects, flowers
Latin American musician playing conga drums at a Salsa Dance
Whales and dolphins
Nuts-bolts-and-tools collage on custodian's door
Peacock with jewels glued on its tail for after-school office
Interpretation of Gaugin women
Original poetry on a scroll
One very talented third grader, chosen by her class, painted her own lazy dragon and disillusioned knight.

Outdoor Wall Mural Painted by Students

A wall mural painted by students is an effective deterrent to graffiti. The paint can be purchased by the PTA, donated by the local paint store or by any other business near the school with an interest in keeping the neighborhood looking good. Local businesses and corporations will often donate money specifically to cover neighborhood graffiti. The students need to work with one or two adult artists—either the art teacher in the school or a qualified parent. Getting as many students involved as possible also helps with discouraging unwelcome graffiti.

Another way to have as many children participate as possible is to put up individual ceramic tiles that the children have painted and glazed on the wall. If the wall is decorated by children it is more likely to remain graffiti-free.

All-School Classroom Cleanup and Campus Beautification Day

This is a good project for early fall, scheduled on a Saturday, all day from 9 A.M. to 5 P.M.. Parents receive flyers or a call from their class parents to come out and work in their child's class. Volunteers come at any time during the day, but most of the classroom work happens in the morning. Usually the teacher supervises; this is a good way for parents to get to know their child's new teacher better.

Make a list with the teacher a week ahead of time of building or cleaning projects and the supplies that will be needed. Have a sign-up sheet for parents to choose the time that is good for them to work, and what items they can bring. Parents bring their own tools and cleaning supplies to make the work go faster. If the whole building is full of activity on the same day, the building maintenance people cannot supply enough hammers, drills, and other tools to go around to everyone. Rent one or two rug-shampooing machines to share if needed. After finishing in the classroom—or if child's classroom teacher doesn't need help that year—parents and kids can work on projects for the whole school. Be creative. Look for every possible idea to improve the school.

Large group projects like installing a ceramic tile mural designed by the children or building a greenhouse or rain shelter can be done on days like this. Invite local volunteer organizations such as the Lions Club, the Chamber of Commerce, the Jaycees, JCC, church groups, or other nonprofit organizations in your area to help with very large projects.

The larger projects will take all day. Shorter projects can be scheduled in the afternoon after the work is finished in the classrooms. Having families bring a picnic lunch to share can make this even more satisfying for everyone.

SAMPLE CLASSROOM LIST

Cleaning and repairing toys, cleaning blocks and the block storage area, repairing classroom books, shampooing rugs, washing windows, dusting window shades and blinds, separating legos and math manipulatives, finding puzzle pieces, reorganizing computer area, removing artwork left over from last year's students.

Building new shelves, cubbies, or storage under or over the classroom sink; paper-towel racks; building display areas for science projects in class; putting up hooks for coats; making cd, tape, and book storage shelves for the teacher's closet; painting; repairing or replacing broken items; tightening all chair and table legs.

Planting: Bulbs, flowers, trees, or shrubs

Raking or clearing: Leaves, trash, or weeds

Repairing: Playground equipment, basketball hoops, painting benches, possibly even sanding and refinishing the gym floor

Building: Rain shelters, a greenhouse, or composting area

Inspecting and replacing: Outside light bulbs and fixtures, sidewalk curbing, crosswalk lines

Painting: Large outdoor murals with the children

Installing inside the school: Bulletin boards or woodstrips to hang children's artwork or projects; cases to display children's art work, woodworking items, or trophies for the whole school

Ceramics Studio

Parents can create a ceramics studio at the school, if there is sufficient demand for pottery classes. Parents should look for a suitable space at the school. Sometimes there are usable rooms that are too small for a regular classroom and too large for a closet, that would be fine for ceramics.

In order for a kiln to be used to fire the children's pottery, the room needs to be wired for 220 volts by a certified electrician, usually one hired by the school system. In some school systems, it is acceptable for a parent who is an electrician to donate his services. A chimney for the kiln will also need to be installed. Of course, a fire extinguisher and fire alarm system are necessary safety precautions.

The room should have heavy-duty shelving for storing pieces before and after firing, and for storing glazes and tools. Parents can volunteer to refinish old tables or purchase new ones for the students to use in class.

Minnesota Clay, located in Minneapolis, Minnesota, is a highly recommended distributor of kilns, pottery wheels, and glazes. They provide excellent service and prices; they can advise parents and teachers on what size kiln to purchase for the school. Developing a relationship with local distributors of clay is better for more immediate delivery once the studio is up and running.

The last ingredient needed is a teacher who has worked with kilns, wheels, and glazes before. Be sure that the teacher has been trained to fire the kiln to the correct temperature for different kinds of clay (porcelain and others) and knows how to stack it properly. The kiln distributor can be helpful in this regard.

MAKE YOUR PLAYGROUND SAFE

Parents are right to be concerned about playground safety. Serious accidents in school playgrounds harm many children every year. If the equipment in your school playground is old, it may not meet current safety standards.

The Parents' Association can hire a safety consultant (or request that the school district hire one) to complete a regular safety audit on the equipment in the playground. The safety consultant will look for many things, such as loose screws, sharp edges, worn or cracking beams and unsafe surfaces under playground equipment. They should also check to see if the playground equipment is age-appropriate.

New or remodeled playgrounds are wonderful for children. If your school is lucky enough to have parents who are willing to design, build, or install equipment, every step still must be reviewed by an safety expert. It is worth the extra time to build and install equipment without known hazards to the children who will use it in years to come.

Work closely with your school district to come up with a plan. There may be funding available from the state, federal or city governments which will pay for the proper safety procedures. Each school is required by law to have a safe playground for the children and some funding should be available.

Websites for Playground Safety

www.uni.edu/playground   This site is the National Program for Playground Safety. It contains regulations and advice.

www.nrpa.org   This site is the National Parks and Recreation/ National Safety Institute. More safety requirements.

www.cpsc.gov   This site is the U.S. Consumer Product Safety Commission. There is information on playground safety here.

RAISING ACADEMIC PERFORMANCE OF STUDENTS

Early Bird Reading Club

Create a reading club that meets before school every morning, so that half an hour to forty-five minutes before school, children can come early and go to the library. Parents or neighborhood volunteers are needed every morning to read to the younger children or help the older ones select books.

In some school systems it is necessary to have a certified teacher or assistant teacher with the children. If that is the case, the PTA can pay an assistant teacher or other certified adult to be in the library every morning to administer the program. If there are more than twenty children, a second adult may be necessary for supervision.

Children must have slips signed by parents or guardians giving permission for the whole year. The sign-up slip should clearly state that any child who cannot follow the rules of behavior can be dismissed from the club.

Volunteer in the Library

During the school day, parent volunteers are needed to shelve books, read to children, and help with research using books or computers. The parent in charge of coordinating the library volunteers can create a sign-up sheet with available times printed on it.

Interested parents can be found through the surveys handed out early in the year. If no one volunteers, the committee chairperson makes phone calls to ask for help.

Create a Reading Tree

This is an old-fashioned, tried-and-true way to encourage kids to read more books. Parents and teachers are always amazed by the response of the children to a reading tree.

First, send home flyers announcing the creation of a Reading Tree. The basic tree without leaves can be cut out of brown construction paper for the trunk and branches. Put it up in a very visible spot in the school where everyone passes it. Children get leaves with their names on them, to put up on the tree when they finish reading the requisite number of books and turn in a form signed by their parents.

In grades K–2, six picture books or one chapter book qualifies a child for a leaf. In grades 3–5, two chapter books are read for each leaf. Winning classes get a pizza party and a library for the class. The reader with the most leaves in each class wins a book. This is one contest everybody wins.

Most of the children get very excited and want as many leaves as possible on the tree. It is important to be very clear about when the contest starts and finishes. A committee of two or three parents, a teacher from grades K–2, and a teacher from grades 3–5 should go over the forms when they are turned in, to be sure everything is in order.

The children can watch the tree grow greener with leaves in the spring—a good time to put up the tree. Winners for each class are given darker leaves with a name written on each leaf. Winners for each division can be indicated by birds with the name of a winner written on them. The birds and darker leaves are put on the tree with all the other leaves, completing the project.

Bookfair to Encourage Reading

Scholastic, Troll, and other children's book publishers can provide a complete book fair for your school. They deliver the books in boxes a couple of days before the fair and pick up whatever is not sold afterward. Hold this event in the library or in any other large room in the school. The company supplies all the books and pays 40 to 45 percent of gross sales. While this is a fund-raiser for the school, it is also a way to show the children that reading books is a valued activity that all the parents in the school—not just their parents—support.

Frequently books from the publishers are expensive. If your school population cannot afford to spend $5 or more on a book at the bookfair, it is sometimes necessary to supplement the books from one company with donated books. Ask for donations before the fair. When each class visits the fair, all the children should be able to go home with at least one book. The donated books can be sold for $.25 to $.50.

The fair usually runs at least three days. Parents are needed to unpack the books, to set up the sale, and to sell during the fair in two-hour shifts. Start before school and end after school each day. If you want to be sure to sell more books, hold the bookfair just before parent-teacher conferences and have the remaining books available for parents to purchase.

Start a Literary Magazine for Kids

Work with teachers to start a literary magazine to be published two to four times a year. You can hold a schoolwide contest to name the magazine. A committee of parents and teachers can select material submitted by teachers from poetry and short stories written by the children in their classes. A certain number of pieces are chosen in each catagory and age group. Printing costs can be donated or paid for by the PTA.

This kind of recognition is invaluable for children who love to see their work in print. It will encourage more children to write, improving both reading and writing skills.

Tutor a Child

Parents can provide important help by tutoring children in reading and math. Some schools restrict tutoring to before or after school. Others allow parents and other volunteers to tutor children in a corner of the classroom or out in the hallway. Usually these volunteers need some basic training, which can be provided by the school district.

It is a good idea to pair each tutor with a teacher and to use tutors who can commit to a regular schedule for the whole year. Volunteers must understand that they are needed on a regular basis in order to be effective. Recruiting tutors can be accomplished in the parent survey discussed in chapter 3.

Add Language Instruction

Your school can enrich the curriculum by encouraging cultural exchange programs set up by the education department in your state. If, for example, your school wanted to start or supplement instruction in Spanish, French, Italian, Japanese, Polish, or other languages, a graduate student could be recruited to come for a year from a foreign country: Students can teach their native language and promote better cultural understanding. They typically live with a family from the school, or the school pays for lodging.

Graduate students are screened by the state education department in New York, and in many other states where education departments have such exchange programs. Check in your state for a similar program or contact the New York State Education Department to set one up.

Special Events in School

BRING A WILDLIFE SPECIALIST TO THE SCHOOL

Contact the local zoo, nature center, or a veterinarian in your area. Ask about whom to contact for traveling petting zoos, snake or birds of prey shows (falcons, hawks, and so on) that could come to the school. Many children have never seen these animals up close before. This sort of event could spark a lifelong interest in the biological sciences.

BRING PERFORMING GROUPS TO THE SCHOOL

Puppet shows, mime shows, musical performers, storytellers, and traveling children's theater troupes can perform in the auditorium. Children's book authors can speak to children or read from their books. Sometimes it helps, in cases of very well-known authors, if the children write letters to the authors through their publishers requesting a visit.

Actors performing historical portrayals (such as George Washington, Emily Dickinson, Napoleon, Mark Twain, William Shakespeare, Booker T. Washington, Martin Luther King, Jr., or local historical figures) can be paid to come to the school. If the school is lucky enough to have parent actors who will perform for free, so much the better. The actors can speak to groups in the library or wander from classroom to classroom, staying in character. Children love to pretend and these kinds of events help make history come alive for them.

Bring in Special Instruction

START A CHESS PROGRAM

Ask members of the local chess club—or parents who can play— to teach the game to interested children. They can establish regular chess classes to teach chess skills during lunch or choice time. Setting up a tournament series and competing with other schools on a regular basis helps students hone their skills and have fun.

START AN INSTRUMENTAL MUSIC PROGRAM

Musical ability is related to math ability; it has also been shown by studies to improve children's concentration. If your school has no instrumental music program, parents may want to sponsor one that could be held before during, or after school, if permitted by the school system.

The program can be started by parents who can teach music or by recruiting music education students from a local college who need experience in teaching. If the school district sees how serious the school community is about having instrumental music, they may find the money to pay for it.

Perhaps the PTA would like to purchase a first set of instruments that stay in school for class use. Students will need to rent instruments for home practice. They can bring the mouthpiece from home to use on the school's instruments. Mail-order companies will rent instruments if no music store exists in the local area. Check the Internet or contact toll-free information for musical instrument rentals at 1-800-555-1212. Another resource is the National Music Educators Association.

START AN ART PROGRAM TAUGHT BY PARENTS

PS 87 in New York City has had a parent-run, volunteer, art-instruction program for more than ten years. Angela Trippi-Weiss, creator and director of Arts-in-Action, says that she and other parents originally hatched the idea when funding for the art teacher at the school was eliminated. Since its inception, this program has grown to fifty-two parent volunteers. Volunteers do not need to be professional artists in order to participate.

Arts-in-Action is a sequential skills development course, which starts in first grade and runs through fifth. Classes are taught twice a month for a double period. This allows the students enough time to get into the lesson in more depth than is possible in a single period; it also creates less frequent interruptions for the classroom teacher.

Parent volunteers receive weekly individual lessons by the director of the program. These parents, in turn, go into the classroom to teach art lessons to the children, equipped with appropriate supplies and source materials. A short period of observation, instruction, and discussion is usually followed by a busy period during which the children produce artwork, under the guidance of the volunteer instructor and the classroom teacher.

The Arts-in-Action program demystifies the process of logical and analytical drawing, enabling every child to learn to draw well. Concepts that are taught include the perception of edges, lines, spaces, relationships, light, color, and shadow. The sequential curriculum moves from one year to the next, building basic skills. The goal of the program is not just learning to draw better because learning to draw better is actually learning to see better, and that awareness is at the heart of the program. This visual awareness, coupled with the children's larger learning experiences, becomes another language for them to use. At the end of the school year, the children's paintings and drawings are displayed on the walls of the school, creating an art show.

The director of the program is paid through a combination of grants and money from the Parents' Association. This program can be duplicated in your school with the right person to direct it and enough interested parents to staff it. It isn't necessary to start with a full program in the beginning. Arts-in-Action started with one second-grade class in its first year and kept adding a class every year as curriculum and staffing were developed. If you would like more information on this program for your school, please contact Angela Trippi-Weiss, Director, Arts-in-Action at PS 87, New York City, 212-678-2826.

Bank Savings Program for Kids

This program is intended to teach kids the value of saving money regularly, and it can improve their math skills. Choose a bank that has a children's savings program. At the beginning of the year have an officer from the bank come to the school to sign children up, and give each child a passbook. Permission cards for the passbook are required, which may be filled out by parents in person or sent home and returned the next day.

Children then bring in one dollar on the same day every week. Each teacher collects the money and turns the weekly collection into the office for safekeeping. Every week or perhaps once a month a parent volunteer collects the envelopes from the office and takes the money to the bank for deposit. The passbooks stay at the bank until the end of the school year, when the students can request their passbooks or leave them at the bank for the following year. If a student continues the program from kindergarten through fifth grade, she will graduate from elementary school with a nice savings account.

To make this simple, hands-on program work, find a local bank that will cooperate and a parent volunteer who is willing to make the deposits on a regular basis. It can be helpful if the parent-volunteer is already a known depositor, or even better, works for the bank. If the bank needs to be sold on the program, bring their attention to the many potential customers—both future and current.

Student Teachers

Having a student-teacher program helps in large public school classrooms. While student teachers cannot match the regular teacher's classroom experience, the more trained adults who can work with the children, the better. The experience is also valuable for the student teachers.

Parents can help establish a student-teacher program by approaching local colleges to bring student teachers to the school for their teaching training. The principal is usually responsible for this, but parents who have contacts with colleges can work with the administration.

Teach for America

A nonprofit organization called Teach for America (TFA) gives college graduates training in teaching. This program was created by founder Wendy Kopp as an emergency solution to a shortage of teachers in rural and urban areas. It provides hands-on experience in goal setting, classroom management, and lesson planning.

For information on how this program might help your school, contact SERVEnet at: http://www.servenet.org/narr_news.html. You can also read the article, "Teacher Corps' Tough Regimen Tasks Recruits," by Jeff Archer in *Education Week*, (1997. 16:[August]:1.).

IMPROVE COMMUNITY SPIRIT INSIDE AND OUTSIDE THE SCHOOL

Teacher and Staff Appreciation Dinner or Breakfast

Show the teachers and staff how much they are valued by hosting a dinner or breakfast in their honor. Survey the teachers and staff to find out whether they prefer a breakfast or a dinner. Send out invitations in advance to ensure attendance and make the event special.

Parents can bring fancy food and flowers to the cafeteria for an evening event. For a breakfast, start serving as soon as the cafeteria is available. Have the cafeteria staff prepare the bulk of the food and coffee. Parents can supplement with fresh fruit, bagels, fresh flowers, and other special items. Then during the meal the PTA president can formally thank the teachers and staff, for all the time and effort they have spent teaching the children that year.

Wish List

PS 87 has a parent-run program called Wish List in which all teachers submit a list of the three or four things they want or need most for the classroom. The Parents' Assocation publishes two of these lists every school year, as a class-by-class listing. The list is sent home to parents who provide whatever they can directly to the teacher who has asked for it: "Mrs. Smith in class 301 needs..." This allows parents to help all the teachers in the school, not just their child's teacher. It also promotes school spirit by involving many parents.

You can ask for donations of goods and services for teachers. Examples of items on teachers' wish lists might include computer printers, paper for the copy machine or computers, special supplies the kids might need for a class project, software programs, aquariums, and convection ovens. A teacher might ask for a volunteer to help with a science curriculum or someone to feed the class pet over vacations.

Newsletter

A school newsletter can be important for communication and can improve school spirit. It can come out monthly or bimonthly and be sent home in children's backpacks to save postage fees. Using a central drop-off point in the main office, a parent can easily be in charge of collecting information for the newsletter.

Newsletters might include monthly calendars, articles by teachers, principals, and parents. Using children's poetry, jokes, and drawings for the newsletter allows children to contribute too. A contest to name the newsletter might yield names like The Backpack News or The Hotline. If a large segment of the parent body speaks another language, like Spanish or Chinese, the newsletter needs to be translated by a parent fluent in both English and the second language. Parents or a local companies may be willing to pay for printing the newsletter.

Directory

For the first edition of a school telephone directory, the parent in charge of the directory can take the emergency cards that parents fill in at the beginning of each school year and enter all the student contact information into a database on a computer. Once all the information is in the database, notices with the student's name and address, parents' name, address, home and work phone numbers for both mom and dad need to be sent home, asking parents to correct any mistakes. Some people have unlisted phone numbers or don't want their addresses printed. On the form that is sent home there should be a box next to each line of the address to check if the parent doesn't want that line to appear in the directory. PS 75 discovered the need for this box from a family in which the father was an undercover cop who wanted to keep his address unpublished.

Include space for two addresses in families with divorced or separated parents. It is also a good idea to create a box to check on the form if school notices are to be mailed to each parent's address in the future.

The directory should be organized by grade, room number, and teacher's name. It should be alphabetized by student last name and include the class parents' contact information. Giving a list of contact information to the class parents before the directory is printed can help get the year organized and off to an easier start for the class parents.

Meanwhile, another parent should be in charge of selling ad space to pay for the directory. Ad pages appear between the class pages, on the inside back or inside front covers. The ads can be divided into different sizes. The smallest—one-eighth of a page—is slightly larger than a standard business card, if the directory is 8½″ × 11″—a convenient size. Next largest is one-fourth of a page, then one-half, and finally, a full-page ad. Different prices work in different parts of the country, typically a full page is usually worth $250 or more, and the smaller ones can be priced accordingly.

Parents in the school who have a business, or just want to wish the students well for the year should be encouraged to buy ads. Send home a notice asking parents to buy ads. Local businesses with a high degree of interest in advertising include car dealerships, print shops, mom-and-pop stores, lawyers, veterinarians, therapists, artists, photo studios, summer camps, music or dance teachers, and karate studios. Restaurants are frequently interested in printing their menus in a full-page ad.

A volunteer to set up the ads will reduce the production costs of the directory. Save time by scanning all the ads onto each page. The cover of the directory can be a drawing by a different child artist every year, or it can simply be a printed title. Make sure the principal and the PTA president can each include a welcome statement in the opening pages. Also include in the opening pages a listing of school phone numbers such as the principal's office, after-school programs, library, guidance counselor, resource room, and special education.

A page should be reserved for all PTA elected officers, committee heads, and school council members with their phone numbers. A "Support our Advertisers" page lists all the advertisers in alphabetical order and formally thanks them. Indexes include: alphabetical student index and parent index (when a parent's last name is different from the student's last name). The directory should include a disclaimer: "At the request of their parents, some children have been omitted from class lists. Any other omissions or errors are strictly unintentional. For these we apologize." It should also include a reminder: "Please remember that the school directory is for personal and school uses only and is not to be used for commercial purposes."

The earlier in the year the directory can come out, the better. The first year of production will take longer, but it becomes easier once the computer contains all the information. Modifications may be made every year, but the bulk of the data entry will include incoming kindergartners and other new students.

Some schools give the directory away free and others hand them out to dues-paying members of the PTA. This is a decision for the PTA to make. The finished product is a great tool for building a community. It is a convenience for the children or their parents when making social arrangements. It is worth the effort.

Earth Day Celebration

Celebrating Earth Day on April 22 every year gives families and the school community a chance to participate in activities to help save the earth. Some possible events include: a display on recycling, making paper from old newspapers, a composting demonstration, and making art from found objects. Or you could organize planting flowers around the school or cleaning up the grounds. You could invite a wildlife specialist to bring animals to show the children.

This is an event the whole family will love. Hold it on a weekend and invite the whole school community, from teachers and staff to grandparents, kids, and friends. An excellent book to use as a guide for the day is *Ecoart: Earth Friendly Art & Craft Experiences for Three to Nine Year Olds,* by Laurie Carlson, which was published in 1993 by Williamson Publishers in Charlotte, Vermont, 1-800-234-8791.

International Night

The spirit of an international night is one of sharing cultures through song, dance, poetry, storytelling, and instrumental performances. It is similar to a talent night, but without the competition and prizes. The purpose is mutual enjoyment and appreciation.

The PTA or School Council must decide on a policy regarding individual performers. While the school wants to encourage children to perform, it is difficult to choose, for example, which child will be allowed to play his piano piece. In order for most of the students to perform, perhaps classes should perform together.

Don't let the show get too long, Establish a maximum length for each act, perhaps five minutes or less.

Variety is another issue. Many cultures and types of acts need to be presented to have a more interesting show. Few people will willingly sit through four different classes performing the same Mexican Hat Dance, unless, of course they have a child in each class!

The planning committee needs at least three months to prepare. In the early stages, survey the teachers to find out if they are interested in helping. Try to have both parent and teacher participation. Assignments for committees include:

Food: Organizes a team to call other parents, asking them to bring ethnic dishes, plates, cups, napkins, juice, soda, water, ice, extra serving spoons, and whatever else is needed for a potluck supper.

Serving: Finds volunteers to help set up and serve the food to families after the show.

Cleanup: It's important to have a crew of volunteers who have committed to help before the night of the event so that the head of clean-up does not do all the work alone.

Director of show: Auditions groups and is a liasion with teachers who want their entire class to perform together. This person reviews what is going to be performed for appropriate content. The director is also responsible for planning the order of the performances, and for scheduling and running rehearsals.

Stage manager: Organizes a plan to get children on and off the stage in a timely manner.

Sound and lighting: Plans the lighting and audio portion of the show, sometimes using older students to help.

Piano player: Usually a teacher or parent can do this job if live music is desired.

Costumes: Designs and makes costumes with the help of parents who sew.

Sets: Art teachers or parents can work with the children to create a backdrop for the entire show.

Announcer: Introduces each act and entertains audience between the different acts. The principal may be a good choice here.

Start the show early in the evening, certainly by six or six-thirty. Be sure the children performing in the show, and the audience, have had a snack beforehand. The show should last no more than one to one-and-a-half hours, leaving time for the dinner afterward. Everyone, including the audience, should be encouraged to come in costumes from other countries. This makes a really colorful and fun-filled evening for all the members of the school. The children in particular love it and learn many things by participating in the show.

Parents love to see their kids perform, to dress up, and to sample new or unfamiliar foods.

Square Dance

Start a new tradition. Have a regular square dance. Hold the event on a Friday night to get the greatest attendance from parents who might go away for the weekend and miss a Saturday-night dance.

First hire a caller. Find one who is a good dance teacher for children. The contra, or line dances, are the easiest for children to learn. Some callers use records and have their own sound systems. Hold the dance in the school gym or any other large room at the school. Keep the price of admission low to encourage everyone to come, but be sure to charge enough to pay for the band.

Selling hot dogs and other dinner food one hour before the dance helps out parents who are coming from work. People can bring food or the PTA committee can buy pizzas or finger food to sell. Start selling food at 6 P.M. and the dancing at 7 P.M.

Make sure to have a number of parents who will round up the young boys or girls at the dance who get bored and start to run around the room. They can be taken to a corner and given something to do if they are not interested in dancing. Square dancing is part of American history and can be discussed in class before the evening of the dance, giving children a chance to learn about an American tradition.

Salsa Dance

Celebrate Hispanic Culture with a Salsa Dance. This evening of Latin American dance could have the same schedule as the square dance, Friday from 7-9 P.M. You will need either a live Brazilian band or a DJ to play the music on equipment set up in the gym. Be sure to find a dance instructor who is good at teaching dance steps to large groups of children. The instructor should know simple versions of the Merengue, Rhumba, Mambo, Salsa, Samba, Macarena, and others. These dances are fun and don't require partners, so they work well with children. Children and their families can wear authentic costumes, if they wish.

Having families prepare and bring rice-and-bean dishes, guacamole, tacos, burritos, nachos, and other types of Spanish or Mexican foods would add another dimension to the experience.

This dance is a great way to honor the Hispanic families in the school. If there are none, it is still a wonderful learning experience for children and their families who have not been exposed to the lively dance culture of South and Central America.

Establish a Working Partnership with Community Organizations

Contact all the nonprofit community-based organizations in the area to find out if any of their members would like to participate in volunteer programs at the school. Put parents in charge of developing relationships with these organizations. The school could create an advisory board—composed of the members of these organizations— to work with the school. Community groups could participate in yearly all-school activities or smaller, more frequent activities.

A listing of local organizations can be found in the telephone directory, but all of the following could be contacted: YMCA, Kiwanis Club, Lions Club, Elks Club, Jewish Community Center, local town recreation centers, JAYCEES, Junior League, churches, synagogues, mosques, local Chamber of Commerce, Masons, Knights of Columbus, square dance clubs.

Volunteers from community groups could help with reading and math tutoring. They could also speak to classes about the type of work they do (careers). They might be interested in cleaning up the school grounds or planting flowers. Or they might prefer interacting with students by chaperoning school trips; performing scientific experiments; teaching art, music, writing; or coaching sports after school.

Community organizations might be willing to sponsor new or

existing programs in the school. Some ideas include taking out ads in the school directory, sponsoring a school play, donating musical instruments, or buying paint for a wall mural designed and painted by students. Be creative: Each of these groups has an area of interest that could be incorporated into a project done at the school.

Senior Citizens Like to Help Children

Some senior centers need activities for the residents who and want to be productive in the community. These older members of the community have time to sit with a child reading a book, drawing, or telling stories from their past. These connections between children and senior citizens are often lost in today's society; these interactions are valuable and need to be maintained.

The school can establish a partnership with a local senior center. The seniors can "adopt" a class and work in various capacities for the whole year. The children can also visit the senior center and get to know all the members. This is a built-in audience for putting on plays, singing, doing art projects together, reading children's stories, and so on.

Corporate Support for Schools

Some corporations sponsor tutoring opportunities. The Subaru Corporation in New Jersy has a special program for employees who would like to tutor children in the public schools. The company allows employees to tutor an hour or two a week at the local school; the schools select students who need the help. This partnership works well for the students, and it is very gratifying for the tutors, who feel they are making a real difference in a child's life.

The John Hancock Insurance Company established a partnership with two Boston elementary schools, The Lucy Stone School and The Samuel Mason School. The partnership was designed so the company could share its resources and expertise with parents and students. Hancock has donated more than a thousand books to the two schools. They have also given globes, maps, computers, and copiers that help meet some basic needs. Teachers and parents have been invited to take part in workshops and training at the company; this has resulted in schoolwide computer training.

Through the Adopt-a-Class program, more than half of John Hancock's vice presidents visit the schools and correspond with the students, which helps build the children's literary skills. The senior officers have made more than twenty visits to the schools and exchanged more than 250 pieces of mail with students. A team from the company and the school working together developed a "Financial Futures" curriculum, which covers the basics of money and finance; this ties John Hancock's business expertise into the partnership. Field trips to the Federal Reserve Bank are another part of this program.

John Hancock is one of fifty companies in Boston that are part of the Boston Private Industry Council (PIC). This group was established in 1979 and has drawn up three Compacts with the city since its inception. The latest Compact, launched in 1995, has six goals: increasing students' access to higher education and employment; developing innovative programs; developing comprehensive curricula; providing training and professional development for teachers; providing support for parents and families; and developing learning centers.

Look around your neighborhood, town or city and find the businesses and corporations represented there. Contact them to find out if a corporate-school partnership already exists in your area. If one does not exist, you could start one, using the Private Industry Council in Boston as a model. Information on the partnership is available from John Hancock Insurance Company: 1-617-572-6000, ask for Public Affairs.

FREE TEACHING MATERIALS AVAILABLE FROM CORPORATIONS

Insurance companies and other large corporations usually have free materials to give to schools and communities. AT&T, for example, wires schools free for access to the Internet. With a little research and a few telephone calls to corporations, parents can supplement the school's curriculum without cost.

State Farm Insurance offers a wide range of materials free to schools on topics about safety for children. Parents or teachers can obtain these teaching materials, including some videos, by contacting a local State Farm Agent. The materials are free for the school. One topic is "Thought, Word and Deed" (K–6), an educational program about building character. Using established lesson plans, teachers help students practice thinking skills and decision making (thought), truthful written and oral communication (word), and constructive, responsible behavior (deed). A video is included in which a "magical" adult helps the children learn to take charge of their own behavior. This program is endorsed by the National Association of Elementary School Principals (NAESP).

Another topic is "Inside Out" (K–6), which teaches health and safety through a whole-person approach to well-being. Prepared lesson plans help students explore internal and external factors that influence health through concepts such as "I am worthwhile," "I am responsible for myself," "I can protect myself," and "I can be careful." An accompanying video contains animated scenes. This topic is endorsed by the NAESP and the American School Counselor Association.

"Smoke Detectives" teaches fire safety to grades K–6. The free kit includes a video, lesson plans, supplementary handouts, a poster, and sheet music. This is one of State Farm's most successful teaching packages and has been endorsed by the NAESP and the International Association of Firefighters.

"Movers and Shakers" is a complete teaching package for kindergarten through 12th grade. It discusses earthquake preparedness. An entertaining video covers the basics of how to make a home safe in case of an earthquake. The free kit also includes lesson plans, supplementary handouts, and a poster. It is endorsed by the NAESP and the Central United States Earthquake Consortium.

Community Uses for School Buildings

The concept of the school as the center of the community can be a powerful one. This can be established by letting a variety of community groups use school buildings, with the approval of the school district. All of the groups who use the school facility will have more interest in preserving and improving it. These groups can pay rent to the school building or barter for the use of the school by working on school volunteer days to beautify or help maintain the school.

PRE-SCHOOLS

Start a pre-kindergarten, nursery school, or Head Start program at the school. The advantages of this idea are many. Parents can give their children a good start before they enter kindergarten, and children will feel more comfortable when they start kindergarten because they have already been going to school there. If it is a Head Start program, federal funds may be available for operating expenses, which will keep the cost low for families.

A well-run preschool provides a service for the community. Beverly Farms Elementary has a very successful pre-kindergarten program, which is well used by the neighborhood children. The more ways a school building can be used for all the members of a community, the more it will be supported by the whole community.

SCHOOL-BASED HEALTH CENTER

A health center for children located in an elementary school can be a welcome collaboration between health professionals and educators. Children need to be healthy to learn and they need to learn how to stay healthy. On-site health services can provide preventive health care, including annual checkups, vision and hearing testing, vaccinations to prevent childhood diseases, nutrition education, and antidrug information. It is helpful for a school to have a nurse on-site. Nurses can administer medication to those students who require it, check for lice, or help in an emergency.

For more information about starting a health center in your school, contact The National Health and Education Consortium at the Institute for Educational Leadership, 1001 Connecticut Avenue, NW, Suite 310, Washington, D.C. 20036. 1-202-822-8405, 1-202-872-4050 (Fax).

COMMUNITY CHORUS REHEARSALS

Start an Intergenerational Chorus, a group of parents, grandparents, children, and other members of the school community who like to sing. Teachers, principals, and support staff are also welcome. You will need a conductor, someone who can play the piano well enough to accompany the group, music, and access to rehearsal space, such as an auditorium. Yearly concerts help build school spirit among the members of the local community.

SQUARE DANCE CLUBS

Sometimes a square dance club needs space for their dances. The school gym or large community room could be rented for a nominal fee or be made available free. It builds good will in the community.

ADULT BASKETBALL LEAGUES

The gyms in public schools are always in demand for amateur basketball games. This sharing of gym space with the adults in the community can bring in rental fees to the school. It brings people to the school and encourages them to give back to the school in other ways.

ADULT EVENING CLASSES

A program of evening classes run at the local school could include literacy programs, college preparation courses, how-to classes, high school graduation test preps (GED), or English As a Second Language (ESL). Hobbies or interests like art, ceramics, sewing, metal or woodshop programs are other possibilities. Classes would have to be approved by the school district and the principal.

MEETING PLACE FOR COMMUNITY-BASED ORGANIZATIONS

Many organizations need monthly meeting space. The local school can provide such space, either for a fee or an exchange of services. Organizations could be contacted to offer meeting space if approval is given by the district office.

READING TREE BOOK LIST
NEW RULES
**K - 2: 6 PICTURE BOOKS OR 1 CHAPTER (INDICATE ON FORM) BOOK;
3RD - 5TH: 2 CHAPTER BOOKS FOR EACH LEAF**

Winning classes get a library for the class and a pizza party; the reader with the most leaves in each class wins a book.

1.) TITLE:_____

    AUTHOR_____ Chapter/Picture_____

2.) TITLE:_____

    AUTHOR_____ Chapter/Picture_____

3.) TITLE:_____

    AUTHOR_____ Chapter/Picture_____

4.) TITLE:_____

    AUTHOR_____ Chapter/Picture_____

5.) TITLE:_____

    AUTHOR_____ Chapter/Picture_____

6.) TITLE:_____

NAME:_____CLASS:_____ GROWN-UP'S INITIALS___

FINAL DAY MAY 16th

3

■ ■ ■

Principals and Parents As Partners

The poor quality of education in many of our nation's public schools makes the daily headlines. Politicians use the need for better schools in their election campaigns. It is a subject that has been analyzed by professional educators for years with mixed success. When a school is failing, officials may blame families or society as a whole, while families point their fingers at the principal or the teachers. However, school administrators across the country have known for years that successful schools count on real grassroots parent involvement. Schools alone cannot educate our children. Everyone has responsibility and must work together: parents, teachers, and principals. But how?

How does a principal allow parents into her office without losing control of the school? "Parent involvement" is on every principal's lips, yet what methods do successful principals use to work with parents for the benefit of the school?

Many excellent ideas can emerge when parents work with the principal. It should come as no surprise that parents want to contribute, particularly because a large number of today's parents are older and bring with them a great deal of life experience. Some have given up jobs in corporations to stay home and raise their families.

Parent leaders are organized, well-educated, and committed to their children's education. As Mary Townsend, PTA President at Findley Oaks Elementary in Duluth, Georgia, put it, "If I wanted to start a new business, I would hire the leaders of our PTA. They are so competent that I never have to supervise them. Give any of them a job or a committee and they make it happen without even talking to me."

Many of today's elementary-school parents have been very active in their children's cooperative nursery school or day-care center. In these preschool centers, parents do everything from painting the walls to serving on the board of directors. These parents are already hands-on participants in their children's education, sharing decisions and accepting responsibility on many levels. A wise principal can tap into the skills and enthusiasm of these active parents.

To begin working with parents as partners, a principal must define for himself the boundaries for parental collaboration. Some of these boundaries are obvious. Decisions about what curriculum to teach, for example, are usually made by the school, not by parents. School districts have policies regarding parent volunteers in classrooms which principals must follow. Some principals are most comfortable with parents' suggestions within the formal structure of a school management council (see chapter 8). A principal sets the tone for the school as a whole, including parent contributions. At the same time, principals need to feel comfortable with parents offering their own ideas, or no real collaboration can occur.

The purpose of having the principal's ear is to come up with ideas to benefit all the children. No principal wants parents who are concerned only with the welfare of their own child. Principals want parents as partners to find creative solutions to problems and to expand the resources of the school through the use of parent volunteers. For this partnership to work effectively, parents must remember that the principal is in charge and responsible for all decisions affecting the school community. It is a very exciting time to be either a principal or a parent in the public schools. Nida Palmore, past PTA President of Manchester GATE Elementary School in Fresno, California summed it up well, "We have a synergy at our school because the principal, teachers, parents, and students work so well together."

HOW PRINCIPALS CAN REACH OUT TO THE SCHOOL COMMUNITY

Communicating With Parents: Establishing a Partnership

Principal-parents breakfast meetings
Home get-togethers with parents
Brainstorming with individual parents
Attending evening school functions
Open door policy for parents
Establishment of parent-active School Management Council
Voice mail or E-mail message system for principal-parent (and teacher-parent) communication
Principal's monthly newsletter
Organize storytelling by parents

Making the School Part of the Community

Create fundraising partnerships with community businesses
Join community outreach programs, such as food drives, coat drives, and so forth
Organize school festivals to include local businesses
Involve organizations such as the Lion's Club, American Heart Association, or the local police department
Be an advocate for the school with community leaders
Invite speakers from local businesses to talk to the children about careers, staying away from drugs and alcohol, or other topics of interest

Working Within the School

Hold an all-school retreat to create a vision for the school's future
Make technology a priority
Create special programs to respond to the needs of all students
Support a strong counseling program
Establish a conflict resolution program, if needed
Work effectively with teachers to support student achievement
Create principal's achievement clubs
Be a visible presence before, during, and after school

STORIES OF PRINCIPALS
AT THE SEVEN SCHOOLS

In this section we will learn from the principal's experiences in each of the seven schools. Each principal has his or her own style of partnering with parents. Each school population is different, which also dictates the dynamics of the principal-parent partnership.

Reinvigorating an Established School

The first example of principal-parent partnership comes from PS 75 in New York City. This school has been the subject of articles in *Family Fun, Family Circle,* the *New York Times,* and the *New York Daily News.* In addition, PS 75 was chosen as a *Redbook* magazine School of Excellence in 1992 and 1994.

ALL-SCHOOL RETREAT

When Roberta Kirshbaum was installed as the new principal of PS 75 in 1989, the parents requested funds from the local school district to hold a retreat. This retreat was designed to get a fresh start and to create a new team for decisionmaking at the school. The retreat was held off-site in a local church community meeting room. It was run by an experienced facilitator recommended by another school district and was open to the principal, parents, teachers, school aides, and assistant teachers. The retreat lasted all day on a Saturday. Lunch and child-care were offered to all participants.

The first activity of the day was discussions by small groups of teachers, parents, and staff about problem areas at the school. Some of the areas needing improvement included the physical plant, the curriculum, and decision making by the administration. Then each group was asked to write a vision or mission statement for the school. Every statement was shared with the combined groups, giving a public forum to people's hopes and dreams for the future of the school. In their last activity, the participants made wish lists: "If our school could have anything, what would we want?" This brainstorming technique stimulated everyone to dream of new possibilities for the school. By day's end, each and every person at the retreat was excited by the positive energy they had generated.

SAMPLE PARENT WISH LIST FROM THE RETREAT
(Yes or No indicates whether implemented later)
Band program for fourth and fifth graders (Yes)
Improved reading and math scores (Yes)
Children's gardening program (No)
New playground equipment (Yes)
Special assemblies: storytelling, wildlife shows (Yes)
New computers in every classroom (Yes)
More supplies in each classroom (varies from year to year)
More trips to museums, aquariums, historical sites (Yes)
Literary magazine (No)
Enriched parent-run after-school program: chess, acting, sports, science, ceramics, computers, Latin, karate (Yes)

An important purpose of holding the retreat was to establish team spirit by setting goals for the whole school community. The participants realized that the whole school belonged to everyone— from its current problems to its hopes and dreams for the future. It became clear that if real change was to occur at the school, it was up to them to do it together. The people who attended the retreat realized that to work together more effectively, they would need an ongoing structure for discussing and solving the problems of the school. The school senate was an outcome of the retreat, created for that very purpose.

CONFLICT RESOLUTION PROGRAM

One issue Mrs. Kirshbaum had to address when she became principal was the need to ease tensions among the diverse student and parent populations that had previously prevented parents, teachers, and students from working together. She explored available ideas and programs and chose one called Resolving Conflicts Creatively. This widely available program trains teachers and parent volunteers to mentor students in effective nonviolent conflict resolution. It worked well at PS 75. This kind of hands-on responsibility made parent volunteers more involved in the daily life of the school.

PRINCIPAL MOBILIZED THE PARENTS

In older schools like PS 75, putting new ideas into operation can be difficult. Parents and teachers are accustomed to things the way they are, whether the situation is good or bad. Change requires a certain amount of optimism on the part of both parents and principal and a willingness to experiment. It also requires a lot of energy and patience.

This school was Roberta Kirshbaum's first job as a principal. She not only approached the job as a challenge, but strongly believed that in time, the school could be returned to its former position as one of the best schools in the neighborhood. She used a cooperative nursery school model, where parents not only have input, but are responsible for supporting the entire school in a hands-on manner. This gave parents a great deal of influence in the workings of the school. It was nothing short of inspirational to parents who wanted to contribute their skills.

She was able to use this new perception of the school—as a place where parents' ideas are important—as a public relations tool to attract even larger numbers of active parents. She gave enthusiastic presentations at neighborhood nursery schools for prospective kindergarten parents, selling the new parent-friendly atmosphere of the school.

PS 75 is in a school-choice district. This means neighborhood families can choose to send their child to any school in the district. The only requirement is there must be a seat available in the school for that child. Consequently, parents shop around. For any school in a choice district to succeed, enough active parents have to be committed to supporting it. Active, involved parents attract more active, involved parents to a school.

MONTHLY PRINCIPAL-PARENTS BREAKFAST

Kirshbaum used many different ways of making parents feel like partners. The monthly Principal and Parents Breakfast helped to accomplish this. This meeting continues at the school, run by Robert O'Brien, PS 75's new principal. The breakfast is an open meeting any parent can attend. It provides all parents with access to the principal, and it helps keep the lines of communication open. At each meeting the principal keeps a list of topics that parents want to discuss and reports on solutions for problems brought up at the last meeting. The only ground rule of the monthly breakfast is that it is not to be a gripe session. Parents bring up concerns and discuss possible solutions. An example of a problem that came up at a past breakfast was the need for supervised games for third-grade recess. As a result, a school aide was hired to organize games and additional play equipment was purchased.

Kirshbaum also understood the importance of recognition for parents. At the end of each school year, she honored parents at a breakfast, presenting them with pins bearing the letters VIP, for Very Important Parent.

VOICE MAIL MESSAGE SYSTEM

Another way parents became partners in PS 75 was through the use of the voice mail messaging system that Kirshbaum had installed in every classroom in the school. The local telephone company asked her permission to use the school as a demonstration site, so the installation and service was free for the first five years.

Each teacher can leave a recorded message for the parents describing what happened in their class for that day. Parents can call from anywhere, listen to the message, and learn what lesson the class studied that day and the homework assignment. Parents can also leave a message for the teacher without taking up class time. This system solves a basic problem for parents: getting the daily information they need without having to interrogate their child every night at dinner. Most children respond to such questions as "What did you do in school today, dear?" with silence or "Nothing, Mom," or "I forget." For this reason, voice mail is very popular with parents and teachers.

ACCESS TO THE PRINCIPAL

In some schools, parents have to schedule an appointment with the principal quite far in advance. Kirshbaum was very accessible, keeping an open door to parents (as is her successor, Robert O'Brien). She met informally with parents in her office to explore new ideas. Her usual response to an idea was "Yes, we can do that." The joke among parents became, "Be sure you want to bring up a new idea because you're going to be the one in charge of making it happen." The principal knew that her parent partners would do whatever was necessary to implement an idea.

An idea that came from brainstorming in Kirshbaum's office was enriching the science curriculum even before the school became part of a National Science Foundation Grant Program. The principal gave approval to the PTA for hiring a science teacher, whom a parent knew by reputation. The self-proclaimed Dr. Dirt came to grades one through five on a weekly basis for two years, conducting hands-on experiments with the children. He also ran an evening of family science in the cafeteria, putting on a very stimulating show for parents and kids.

PRINCIPAL AS ADVOCATE FOR PUBLIC SCHOOLS

During her six-and-a-half years at PS 75, Roberta Kirshbaum was an articulate, intelligent principal who used her communication skills to speak to parents' hearts. She persuaded middle-class parents to send their children to PS 75 instead of other schools in the district. Her argument that you shouldn't try to shelter your children from diversity resonated with neighborhood parents.

Kirshbaum developed a close working relationship with the district superintendent, constantly pushing for more resources. She directed media attention—local television stations, newspapers, magazines, and book publishers—to PS 75. A series of articles in the *New York Times* about teaching reading to third graders resulted in thousands of book donations to the school from all over the country.

She established relationships with many of the world-class cultural institutions that New York City has to offer, like the Museum of Modern Art, the Little Orchestra Society, the Chekov Theater, Carnegie Hall, Elliot Feld Ballet, the Joyce Theater, Ballet Hispanico, and Western Winds Vocal Ensemble.

She persuaded local groups to help the school. A private foundation sponsored by an individual in the neighborhood put hundreds of books in the school library. The library was completely remodeled through funds from the Lila Acheson Wallace Power Library Grant program. The Sterling Foundation, a community volunteer organization, received approval from Kirshbaum to organize a community work day at the school and, along with parent volunteers, built a rain shelter on the playground for parents waiting to pick up their children. With assistance from volunteers, the art teacher hung a painting created by a group of children 120 feet by 20 feet on the side of the building overlooking the K–2 playground. New York Cares, a not-for-profit volunteer organization, planted hundreds of donated tulip bulbs around the school.

Kirshbaum also established a relationship with the Jewish Community Center of the Upper West Side. They then created a reading and tutoring program called The Gift of Literacy. In this program adults tutor children who need help with reading either before or after school on a one-to-one basis. This tutoring program continues in the school and has helped many students since its inception.

STORYTELLING BY PARENTS

The principal used other innovative methods to make parents a part of the school beyond the usual fund-raising and tutoring. One example was bringing in a Cornell University program called Confabulation, or Family Stories. In this program parents and grandparents came into their child's class and told stories from their family history and the "old country." Sharing these stories with the children made the parents feel like part of the school family. One story I found especially moving was told by an Egyptian mother who remembered, as a child, throwing her favorite doll into the Nile River as part of a ceremonial ritual. She didn't realize what she had done until she saw her doll floating away forever and she began to cry.

Another storytelling project from the principal was called Read-Aloud Day in Riverside Park. Parents, teachers, and district-office personnel volunteered to dress as characters from a book they had chosen to read to a class of children. Classes from kindergarten through fifth grade participated. Each reader stood under a tree in Storyland with a sign numbered for their assigned class and waited for the children to find them. The readers' costumes were colorful and funny, making the stories come to life. Read-Aloud Day became an annual event and Kirshbaum always dressed up for the occasion.

One year she was Pippi Longstocking, another time, the Cat in the Hat, another, Amelia Bedelia.

Since Kirshbaum has gone, the school families have welcomed O'Brien as the new principal. He has many good ideas on curriculum and organization that are having an impact on the school. He is also aware of the positive relationship the parents enjoyed with the previous principal and wants the collaboration to continue. This is good news for the future of PS 75.

Georgia Principal Tries New Ideas

Sadie Etris has been the principal at Findley Oaks Elementary School since the school opened in 1993. She is a lifelong resident of the area, who has taught and worked in Fulton County Schools for twenty-four years. She started her career as a first-grade teacher, moved up to seventh grade, became an assistant principal, and then a principal at another school prior to opening Findley Oaks Elementary. This principal's philosophy is simple but sound: "If it's good for kids, we're going to do it." This includes experimenting with new ideas. If these experiments succeed, they are retained. If not, they are discarded.

One successful experiment is the Morning Song. The principal makes announcements over the loudspeaker every morning. After the announcements, one of five or six songs, such as "Fifty Nifty United States," is played over the loud-speaker. The children look forward to guessing which song will the Morning Song that day. Since the Morning Song has been such a success, Etris has added a half hour of classical music before announcements. The tapes are selected by the school's orchestra teacher, Clare Mansell. From 7:20 A.M. to 7:50 A.M., while the children are arriving and going to their classrooms, classical music is played over the loudspeaker system. It creates a calm start to the school day. Scientists have repeatedly discovered classical music improves mood and helps people perform intellectual tasks.

Since becoming the principal of Findley Oaks, Etris has developed an excellent working relationship with parents. She encourages parents to contribute and then delegates many tasks to them. She considers the PTA committee chairpersons to be ambassadors for the school. Both the principal and PTA President Mary Townsend say that parents view their role at Findley Oaks as "the frosting on the cake." The school would survive without help from the parents, but it would not be as wonderful as it is with their help.

Parents know Etris is available if her door is not closed, and the PTA committee members feel free to walk in to talk with her. Meetings are usually short, and always to the point. Etris welcomes and listens to parents, looking for ideas that will benefit the children. She says she can accomplish more informally in her office with parents than at formal meetings. Parents appreciate her willingness to include them in so many aspects of the school experience.

Etris stands on the curb in front of the school every morning and afternoon to welcome and dismiss students. This allows her to connect, if only briefly, by waving to the parents who drop off their kids. If any parent needs to speak to her, she is available to them for a quick word or to set up a meeting at a later time.

KEEPS PARENTS INFORMED

Every other week Etris sends out her own newsletter, called the *Findley Flyer,* highlighting school activities. This newsletter keeps parents informed of upcoming programs such as a parenting workshop, run by the counseling department at the school, or other family activities.

To make sure that children and parents have an easier start to every school year, Etris makes sure that Findley Oaks participates in Sneak Preview, a program created by the county school system. The parents and children get to meet and talk to the child's new teacher and see the new classroom during the week before school officially opens. At the Sneak Preview PTA representatives hand out volunteer forms and information. Everyone has lunch in the Food Court, which is the new name for a school cafeteria, and gets to know their new classmates. This meeting helps with transition on the first day of school.

Etris is a person who takes quick action for her school, but also works very closely with parents. She and the parents of Findley Oaks have formed an effective team.

PARTNERS WITH COMMUNITY BUSINESSES

Etris initiated a partnership with a local business that benefits the school. This is part of a program developed by the Fulton County School System. A Mailboxes, Etc. store gives a cash rebate to the school, based on parent purchases. It is especially lucrative at Christmas and other holidays when parents mail a lot of packages. This program could serve as a model that very easily could be set up in other parts of the country.

Etris also makes sure that Findley Oaks participates in the local Kroger and Publix supermarkets' Parents Cash Card program. The parents shop at one of these two markets, and when their purchases reach $150,000 at Kroger or $75,000 at Publix, the school receives a check for $500 from that store. Parents show a computerized cash card, which is scanned, and the market keeps track of the amount of purchases by the parents. The supermarkets support the schools and keep public school parents as loyal customers. This program is an excellent fund-raiser for the schools, so Etris and the PTA both encourage parents to shop for groceries at these stores on a regular basis.

Kentucky School Has Smooth Transition to a New Principal

The reason Dry Ridge Elementary School is such an award-winning school has a lot to do with the former principal, Nancy Duley. She was at the school for seventeen years, first as a regular classroom teacher, then as a special-education teacher. She moved up to assistant principal and was principal of Dry Ridge for six years. She felt strongly that "you have to be a team player."

Many Dry Ridge parents work full-time and are not available during the day. Because of this, she felt strongly that the school had to take on more responsibility for rearing and educating the children. Most of Dry Ridge's children are bused to school, so the principal doesn't have daily opportunities for quick discussions at the beginning or end of the school day. "It is very important for the school to have regular communication with parents," she says. Duley made this communication happen. Each teacher sends home a newsletter in the children's backpacks every Friday, detailing the homework and spelling words for the following week, plus any announcements. Every quarter, the school mails home a newsletter reminding parents to check the backpacks on Friday.

In 1997 Duley moved on to a school in another county and Constance Deats became principal. Before becoming a principal, Deats had extensive experience as a facilitator for school-management councils throughout the state. Because of this experience, she brings a wealth of information to her role as a principal and member of the school-management council. More information on the Dry Ridge Council is included in chapter 8.

Helping the families and children of Dry Ridge is very important to Deats. She is concerned about parents' attendance at curriculum night and other school-sponsored evening meetings and carefully schedules them so working parents will be able to attend. If necessary, she makes home visits to families to discuss their children's development.

Deats already knew the families of Dry Ridge, having worked closely with Nancy Duley on several school projects. This has made the transition to a new principal go more smoothly for the entire school.

Maryland Principal Keeps Up a Dialogue With Parents

Laura Siegelbaum has been the principal of Beverly Farms Elementary School, in Potomac, Maryland, since 1993. She is proactive in her relationship with parents, most of whom devote many hours to the school. When she first became principal, Siegelbaum held a series of principal's evening coffees at parents' homes. The purpose of these get-togethers was "to break down the mystique" of having a new principal. She asked parents at that time to "let me know what you're thinking."

She answered their questions in a very honest way, promising to get back to the parent if she did not know the answer at that time. And then she did, showing that she respected a parent's need to know.

Even though she has been at the school for a few years, she still feels that one of her most important jobs is to talk directly with parents about their concerns. She keeps her ear to the ground and is alert to dealing with problems before they become insurmountable. She is very aware that the parents of Beverly Farms have high expectations in terms of what they want for their children, what they expect from them, and what they can expect from the school for their tax dollars.

FORMAL COMMUNICATION WITH PARENTS

Siegelbaum attends all PTA meetings in the evenings and gives a monthly report. She writes her own weekly newsletter for parents and teachers. In it she reminds parents of important events and meetings for the week. She also recognizes the volunteer efforts of parents in the school. Siegelbaum frequently reports on fund-raising efforts, including the Giant Supermarket "cash-register receipts for computers" program. In one of her newsletters last year, she offered an unusual incentive to encourage parents to bring in their receipts. If parents turned in a certain large number of receipts, she promised to kiss a pig on Valentine's Day. They turned in the required number, and Siegelbaum delivered on her promise, much to the delight of the children.

TECHNOLOGY IS A PRIORITY

Siegelbaum strongly supports parents' efforts to have the latest computer technology installed in the school. In the spring of 1997 she made sure that the school was wired for the Internet as part of the governor of Maryland's Net Weekend. This was a volunteer effort by members of the community, including local contractors and parents. The parents, with the principal's help, are working on getting a computer, printer, and scanner for every classroom and creating a lab with all new computer equipment.

Siegelbaum makes sure that all support services provided by the county school system are working for the children. One such service is the counseling program at Beverly Farms run by school counselor Sherry Satin. Satin runs a comprehensive program and is a popular figure in the school. She is sometimes called a "substitute mom" by students, who ask for her help by leaving notes in the pink flamingo mailbox on her door. She meets with each class, kindergarten through fifth grade, from six to eight times a year, offering guidance for developmental issues and preventative counseling.

Satin works with kids both individually and in small groups on such issues as teasing, bullying, friendship, peer pressures, self-esteem, separation, and divorce. She runs a special program for ADD children, which uses techniques such as "putting on the brakes." She helps children problem solve and take action in situations where they need help.

Satin's peer mediation program has trained students to be on the Talk-It-Out team. These older children walk around the playground with walkie-talkies to help resolve conflicts among children. They help children use words instead of fists. The mediators give children who are involved in conflict with another child Talk-It-Out Tips that can quickly solve a dispute.

Siegelbaum is a principal who is very aware of her responsibility to the parents and children of Beverly Farms. She takes her relationship with the parents very seriously and makes sure that children have the proper resources available to help them learn and grow. Siegelbaum clearly has the childrens' best interests at heart.

California Title 1 School Has a New Principal

Richard Morgan is the new principal of Wesley Gaines School. He is new to the school, having become principal in July 1997 and is continuing all of the programs put in place by his predecessor, Susan Lance.

One of these programs is called Principal's Club. This is recognition from the principal for individual students who want to excel in grades K–5. In each grade students come into the principal's office and demonstrate that they have the knowledge required to be a member of the Principal's Club. Kindergarten children must know the alphabet. First graders read a selected passage aloud. Second graders show off their math facts. Third graders are required to recite the multiplication tables from 1 through 12. Fourth graders demonstrate a knowledge of division. Fifth graders pass a test in word problems, called mental math. Each child who passes the test is then awarded a certificate of achievement and membership in the Principal's Club for their grade.

The principal works with district specialists to host parenting workshops that are held once a year for Gaines's parents. The workshop is actually held twice, once in English and again in Spanish. Each workshop is a six-week series of classes, which are well attended by parents.

Richard Morgan described another program for the students called Gaines Grizzly Days. This is a day of special activities held once a month. It is designed to change the daily routine for the children and give them a chance to choose an activity themselves. The teachers offer a class about their own interests such as music, art, drama, or sports. The kids then choose one of the special classes which are held after lunch and last one-and-one-half hours.

Morgan is proud of the Reading Recovery program at his school. The local school district trained a teacher to be a Reading Recovery trainer. This trainer has in turn trained many teachers at Gaines. The children who needed early intervention to boost their reading have benefited from this program. Teaching reading is one of the great strengths of Gaines School.

The school maintains a computer lab with twenty Power Macintoshes. All students use the lab to learn basic computer skills. The lab has a connection to the Internet and is well supervised by teachers.

The principal sends out a weekly parents' newsletter, which includes announcements and items of interest to parents. He also encourages parents to participate in campus beautification projects such as graffitti removal and planting shrubs and flowers.

Wesley Gaines is an award-winning school. The principal of this large school pays attention to keeping it that way. Even though Richard Morgan is new to the school, he has already made parents a priority in the education of their children.

Hawaiian Principal Enjoys Being Member of the Community

Jules Ino of Kula Elementary School in Maui, Hawaii, has been at the school since 1991. A very dynamic principal, he works closely with the school as well as the community. Ino is friendly and open in his relationships with parents. Like other successful principals, he welcomes students in the morning and dismisses them in the afternoon as they get on school buses. He stands in front of the school, greeting parents as they drop off and pick up their children.

Ino says, "The role of the PTA is to support teachers and staff in achieving our mission of educating children for the twenty-first century." He adds that "being open to the research and leadership of the school is important for parents." He also recognizes that the school needs to be open and receptive to the ideas of the PTA.

Ino makes sure that the school works with many volunteer community organizations. The Lions Club supports the school guidance program. Community health organizations like the American Cancer, Lung, Heart, and Diabetes associations all provide information and support to the school. Teachers work with the police department in the Drug Awareness Program, in which a police officer provides classroom instruction for fifth-grade classes.

The principal also keeps track of the efforts of parents and other volunteers. Here is typical list of what took place during the months of January and February 1997. It is clear from this list that the principal coordinates and depends upon the efforts of the adults in the community.

2	volunteers: working one-on-one with special problem kids
25	volunteers: school campus beautification, school plays, awards, class parties, and so on
1	volunteer: community enhancement and welcoming new parents and visitors
40	volunteers: tutoring
30	volunteers: teacher assistance
100	volunteers: supervision on the playground and field trips
2	volunteers: clerical work in the office
4	volunteers: assisting in fund-raising
1	volunteer: public relations
4	volunteers: newsletters and flyers

CONNECTED TO THE WORLD BEYOND THE ISLANDS

Ino is very computer-savvy, communicating by E-mail with people all over the world. He connects his small community with events and resources on the mainland through the use of the wide-area network in the school. An example of such a collaboration is Kula School's partnership with the Kennedy Arts Foundation in Washington, D.C. Professionals from the Foundation teach the students performing arts, such as dance and acting, using distance learning. Another partnership with the local Maui Arts and Cultural Center allows the school to work on an intergrated approach to the arts and regular curriculum areas like reading, language arts, and social studies.

Ino's favorite school activity is the Harvest Festival, which involves many community members and personal friends. He is the coordinator of this huge event, scheduling and organizing all the activities and people involved. Thanks go to Alan Kaufman, a past PTA president at Kula, for the description of the festival that follows.

The annual Kula School Harvest Festival takes place in the fall and raises most of the money needed by the school for the year. It is a very colorful event and is a true coming together of the community. Teachers, parents, and administrators all donate a minimum of two hours, usually on the first Saturday of November, to provide the needed people power. Tents go up on the playground the day before, put there by the principal and the work crew of parents and other community members Ino has assembled. Entertainment, all performed by volunteers, takes place throughout the day: Musical groups sing, dancers dance, a karate club may perform. Frequently, the entertainment demonstrates the wonderful ethnic diversity of the community. In a single day one can be treated to hula, African dance, a Portuguese dance ensemble, and Master Holland's Tang Soo Do Korean Karate.

The food booths are up and running all day. All kinds of food are sold, from coffee and pastries to shaved ice, chili and rice, spam musubi (a Hawaiian specialty), sushi, and Korean barbecue. Ethnic diversity is reflected again in the range of available delicacies.

The bookstore is open all day. Year after year it has proved very successful, selling donated books for children and adults. Local produce is sold at the country store, and people come early for the fresh fruit and vegetables that have been donated by the farming community. Crafters rent space to set up their booths, which feature glass blowing, jewelry, clothing, and other items of interest.

The Brownies run the shaved-ice stand. The parents partner with them so that they get to keep half of the profits for their group. Pony rides and mini horse-cart rides are offered all day, unless heat or fatigue sets in first. The lines for these rides never end.

Game booths are set up, featuring activities like basketball toss, bean-bag throw, sandbox dig for treasure, plastic fish pond/win a prize. These activities keep the younger children busy. A local entrepreneur, known as the Waterman, rents the PTA his Bouncing Castle and other large toys at nonprofit rates. This is where the older children burn off their energy.

Scrip or tickets are purchsed at central locations for use at the booths. A local security service volunteers its services, and that of its German Shepherd, to retrieve money for delivery to the PTA treasurer for accounting and then deposit in the safe.

Volunteers include: parents, aunts, uncles, grandparents, teachers, and members of the community without children in the school. One year the PTA ran short of volunteers; it happened to be an election year, and Ino and the other festival facilitators turned to politicians and candidates for help. The response was excellent. The organizers made it a policy that no distribution of campaign literature would be allowed, but hats and T-shirts with campaign slogans and names were permitted.

A live auction is also part of the Harvest Festival. Thousands of dollars worth of items are donated every year by the island community. These gifts include luxury-hotel stays, sailing trips, whale-watch trips, bicycle rides, lunch (or an afternoon of snorkeling) with a teacher, art work, rice pots, CDs, haircuts, makeovers, income-tax preparation, graphics design time, secretarial work, livestock, animal supplies and treatment, and more.

This type of harvest festival in an elementary school is familiar to many parents. Kula, like all schools, has its own distinctive foods, booths, and most of all, community involvement. In this small town, this is the kind of involvement that principal Ino thrives on.

In the fall of 1997, Ino started a leave of absence. While he was gone, the school continued its regular programs and activities. It is a tribute to him that everything has run smoothly. The school community is looking forward to welcoming him back.

Principal Is Sports Coach at Manchester GATE

Russ Painter is the principal of Manchester GATE, a gifted and talented school in Fresno. Painter is an enthusiastic, straightforward person, proud of the students in his school and their many accomplishments. This is a hands-on principal. In addition to his duties as principal, he is in charge of coaching the boys' sports teams: football, basketball, softball, cross-country, and track. He shares this activity with his vice principal who coaches the girls' teams.

Painter believes in "management by walking around" and is a visible presence on school grounds. He even directs traffic every afternoon at dismissal, making sure that the eleven buses and all the students walking to meet their parents are safe. The school is located at a busy intersection where the traffic comes from three directions.

His office has the desk pushed against the wall so that meetings with parents, students, or teachers can be face-to-face. He doesn't want any obstacles in the way when speaking with others because direct and immediate communication is his priority. When he gets a call from a parent, he always tries to call back within the hour.

Painter believes that one of his jobs is to show parents how wonderful Manchester really is. At Back-to-School Night he meets with the kindergarten through second- grade parents and the third-through fifth-grade parents separately. During each meeting he gives a vision for each age group for the school year. Parent conferences, which are held in November, have a 95 percent attendance rate at Manchester.

He is very proud of the music program at the school, which includes orchestra, band, chorus, and jazz band. These groups perform in the local area at events such as the Fresno Mardi Gras celebration. They also perform at school for the parents.

Painter is always arranging concerts performed by the children or other programs of special interest to parents to get them to come to school. Once they come in, he believes they become advocates and volunteers. He knows that the support of parents is essential to keep the school running at such a high level, and he encourages parents to take the ball and run with it.

He sends home his weekly newsletter, called the *Parent Pak*, every Monday in the children's backpacks. This contains weekly announcements to the parents. The *'Gator Grapevine* is the students' monthly newspaper. The students write the articles, stories, and poetry, and the principal edits the paper. He also writes a "Principal's Message" column on topics of interest to parents and students. He will also makes copies of flyers for the PTA when they are needed.

Painter believes another of his jobs is removing obstacles for teachers, parents, and students to improve the quality of learning. He is really a facilitator in the truest sense of the word. As one way to meet the demands of a constantly changing world, he is starting a summer program for students at the school called the Manchester Academy of Math, Science, and Technology. This program will be available to any student who is interested in participating.

The school was chosen as a Best Schools in America, *Redbook* magazine award-winner for the state of California in 1995. Painter, the teachers, and parents have created a dynamic school that is a model for schools in its own state and around the country.

4
■ ■ ■

How to Get Parents to Volunteer

An active, organized parents association is necessary to accomplish education goals. If your school does not have an active Parent Teacher Association or has one that could use some new life, you will find this chapter useful. The first ingredient you need for an active parents association is *parents*. You need to attract enough active parents to support the school.

In every parent body there are three basic groups:

1. A small group of active parents will show up, no matter what. These people keep the Parents' Association running and are the ones who always come to meetings. Sometimes it seems to them that they are the only ones who ever do anything for the school. If there are too few of these parents in your school, they will burn out very quickly and may become too tired to try new ideas.
2. A second group is parents who might volunteer if an activity could fit into their busy schedules or was something they could

do from their place of work. This group also includes parents who have a special talent or expertise that could be tapped.

3. The third and largest group will never participate, no matter what you do to encourage them. They will come to social events, perhaps, and they often have very legitimate reasons why they can't be more involved. They should always be included in school events and encouraged to participate.

The second group is the one to go for. If you can attract more people from the second group and combine them with the people from the first group, you will have a larger PTA, one which can work in more ways to support teachers and students.

SOCIAL EVENTS HELP WITH COMMUNITY BUILDING IN THE SCHOOL

Among the many reasons people are attracted to a volunteer organization like the PTA is to be helpful and have fun. Social events like a potluck dinner or bake sale are fun for everyone; they can draw people into the PTA. They also raise money and strengthen a sense of community among parents. Parents are more likely to respond favorably to a request to volunteer if they have met other parents and feel comfortable with them.

Building a strong school community is an essential part of supporting our schools. The more contact parents have with each other at school events, the better they can relate to each other and the school community as a whole. Sharing the common experience of raising children can create a strong bond among parents. Parents often like to report good news or are relieved to hear that another parent is having the same problem they are having, or may already have a solution. It is reassuring to parents to know that they have a built-in support system from other parents in the school community.

The feeling of belonging to the school community can also create a sense of ownership and responsibility that is invaluable in a volunteer organization like the PTA. Working together for the good of the school is a natural outcome of feeling that you belong to the community. It can also encourage parents to support the whole school as part of a team, not just as a volunteer only in their child's class.

Welcome Party for New Students

Before students even enter school in the fall as new kindergartners or first graders, the PTA can welcome children and parents with a party. One easy way to do this is to have a Popsicle Party, giving popsicles to the children and parents who want them. Whatever you do, the purpose of the party is to make the children feel comfortable at their new school. It is also a great chance for parents to meet each other as members of the PTA hand out popsicles and sell school T-shirts. Parents and children get their first opportunity to talk to other new parents and students, and to begin the process of bonding with the school community.

This is the new parent's first exposure to the PTA, and it is important to include them and make them feel as comfortable as possible. Hand out information on after-school programs. Be sure to have the principal speak and introduce the kindergarten and first-grade teachers. The PTA officers can greet new parents and show them how important new families are to the school.

The Most Important PTA Meeting of the Year

Early every fall, most schools hold a Curriculum Night (also called Back-to-School Night) at which each teacher sits down with the parents and explains the curriculum for the year. The PTA can capitalize on this event by holding a large PTA meeting in the auditorium immediately following the classroom meetings with the teachers. At this meeting, parents vote on the PTA budget for the year, and committee heads make appeals for volunteers. Parents fill out those all-important survey forms, which will be used all year by PTA committees. To make it easier for parents to attend curriculum night and the meeting, the PTA should provide childcare at the school.

This evening meeting is the time to get together with other parents and volunteer for committees. Most people are enthusiastic, fresh from summer vacation and ready for action at school. PTA officers and committee heads mingle with new parents and old parents, establishing fresh connections. If you can't get parents to volunteer at this meeting, chances are you won't be able to get them for the rest of the year.

SELECTION OF CLASS PARENTS

During the curriculum meeting in each classroom, classroom parents are elected (see illustration 120A). Classroom parents provide vital links between teachers, other parents, and the PTA. Their duties include: helping with arrangements for class trips or projects; acting as liaison between the teacher and other parents; and creating a phone tree among the parents in the class. A phone tree is a daisy chain of phone calls set in motion when the first person calls a set number of assigned people who then each call a small number of people. It is a quick shortcut for calling everyone in the class in one night.

The classroom parents are an important link in successfully involving other parents in school activities. One parent, the class representative coordinator, coordinates all the classroom parents for working on events like Classroom Cleanup and acting as a link with the PTA.

PARENT SURVEY FORMS

Many parents have work or home skills that can be useful at the school and would like to volunteer when their schedules permit. Working parents may be able to make phone calls in the evening, but could not help out at any event during the day. How can the Parents' Association find out who can do what and when they can do it?

Parent-survey forms are a basic tool for an effective non-profit organization like the PTA (see the Parents Association Survey on page 92). When the parents enter school for the first time to register their child, in addition to filling out an emergency card, each

PARENTS' ASSOCIATION SURVEY

PLEASE FILL THIS OUT NOW AND RETURN IT TO PTA BOX IN
MAIN OFFICE OR BRING IT TO THE NEXT PTA MEETING

COMPLETE one form for EACH FAMILY:

Parent or Guardian's name: _____
Parent or Guardian's name: _____
Child(ren): _____
Grade/Teacher(s): _____
Home address: _____
Home phone: _____ Work phone: _____ Work
Phone: _____
Fax Line: _____ E-mail address: _____
(Do I check my E-mail regularly?) (Y) _____ (N) ___✓___
Parent Occupation: _____ Company: _____
Parent Occupation: _____ Company: _____

I CAN VOLUNTEER DURING THE DAY: _____ hours _____ or, at night:
_____

I WOULD LIKE TO PARTICIPATE IN THE FOLLOWING:
Please check off as many as you can.

___✓___ Reading Volunteers—at a consistent time during school
_____ International Night
___✓___ Auction
___✓___ Square dance
___✓___ Salsa dance
_____ Spring Carnival
_____ All-School Clean-up Day
___✓___ Election Day Bake Sale
___✓___ Gift Wrap Sale Committee
___✓___ Magazine Sale Committee
_____ Parent Tours
_____ Library help
_____ Bookfair
_____ School Photos
_____ Assisting art teacher
_____ Newsletter monthly Spanish translation
_____ Antibias Committee
___✓___ T-shirts
___✓___ Technology Committee
_____ Classroom parent coordinator
_____ Staff Appreciation Dinner
_____ Grant Writing

_____ Spanish/English classes for parents
_____ After-school Committee

I HAVE SKILLS AND/OR EXPERIENCE IN THE FOLLOWING AREAS:

_____ graphic design
_____ live translation for meetings Spanish ____ Chinese ____
_____ written translation Spanish ____ Chinese ____
_____ storytelling
_____ puppet shows
_____ musical theater

DONATION OF SUPPLIES AND SERVICES:
I have access to the following that I could donate:

_____ copy paper (8½ x 11″)
_____ art supplies
_____ printing of school phone directory
_____ musical instruments: what kind? _____
_____ computer printers/scanners
_____ educational software for MacIntosh or IBM PCs
_____ books for classroom libraries
_____ blank cassette tapes for the music teacher
_____ rugs for classrooms

CORPORATE DONATIONS
Our PTA has nonprofit status, 501(c)3. Companies or individuals can receive a tax write-off for donations of money or goods.
I have contacts at a foundation or corporation who might be able to help the school ____ (Y) ____ (N)
If so, who are they? _____
Company _____ Phone Number _____
My company may have a corporate nonprofit donation policy ____ (Y) ____ (N)
Is it a matching policy? ____ (Y) ____ (N)

AUCTION DONATIONS GO ON ALL YEAR
I can or I have friends who may be able to donate goods or services that the school can use or sell at the auction ____
What kinds of things? _____

I have a station wagon, large car, or van which could be used to transport goods if needed this year ____

Thanks for taking the time to fill out this survey. Please call me if you have any questions.

PTA President

P.S. 75 CLASS PARENT DESCRIPTION

A committed, dependable, selfless person, possibly having halo, wings or magic wand, who likes talking with other parents. Able to communicate effectively and listen well. Willing to make a few phone calls. Unable to say "no."

(1) Set up telephone "tree" within classroom to get information to all parents as quickly and efficiently as possible.

(2) A positive attitude about the events you are asked to solicit help for is paramount. Remember, more bees are caught with honey...

(3) The P.T.A. depends on class parents to make sure that each parent in each classroom is contacted about each individual event. Without your support, events will not reach their full potential.

(4) Communicate needs and/or requests made by teacher to all parents. For example, if teacher needs supplies, i.e. cardboard boxes for a specific class project: your job will be to get the parents in your class to bring in cereal boxes, shipping boxes, etc. for their needs. Other classes may have a class fund. Your job would be to collect it.

Your role is vital in the makeup of our school. Our children need you. We need you.

---

parent can fill out a survey form for the PTA. These survey forms should also be filled out at the first large PTA meeting in the fall for returning families. The survey asks basic questions such as times that a parent could volunteer, skills the parent could offer to the school, and both parents' occupations. The sample survey form included at the end of this chapter can be copied as it appears, or be modified to fit your school's needs.

These forms can be kept in the office in the PTA file drawer or in a convenient place where all officers, committee heads, members, or teachers can have access to them. This makes it faster to find volunteers when they are needed; it also more effectively involves more parents, based on their interests and skills.

SCHOOL PHONE DIRECTORY

Communication among parents is essential to support the activities of the PTA. A school directory is an essential tool to foster communication among parents. A student telephone directory helps create a sense of community within the school.

Organize it by class and include the name, address, and phone number of each child in the class. List class parents under the teacher's name. Computers really make this kind of book very easy to maintain from year to year. It does require time to enter the data, but it becomes easier after the first year since most students remain in the school. Make the school directory free to all families, if possible, or perhaps with a membership in the PTA. Distribute it early in the school year. It can be financed by selling advertising to local merchants, and to parents in the school. Many neighborhood merchants will want to renew their ads every year. Parents are their potential customers, so it isn't hard to get merchants to advertise. Pages can be divided into as little as one-eighth of a page to keep the price affordable. Selling ads takes time, but it is a nice way to acknowledge the businesses and parents who support the school while making money at the same time. A business or parent could, of course, pay for the reproduction of the whole directory, if your school has such an benefactor.

SCHOOL NEWSLETTER

Another good communication tool is the school newsletter. A school newsletter can be maintained by a parent and includes announcements, news of interest to parents and children, and the monthly calendar. If your school has a large Spanish-speaking, French-speaking, Chinese-speaking, or other non-English-speaking population, everything must be translated. Recruit one of the bilingual parents to translate the newsletter.

Send the newsletter home in the children's backpacks to avoid mailing costs. A parent's employer could be asked to donate the copying costs each month. In addition to the newsletter, the PTA can send home flyers announcing special events in two languages. Putting up colorful signs in the school reinforces your information about meetings and events.

A final word about communication. It may take extra effort to make sure everyone knows what the PTA is doing in terms of activities, meetings, and voting on budgets. One effective way is to use a copy machine or scanner to enlarge meeting notes to three feet by two feet and attach them to the walls of the school lobby to make them impossible to miss.

Communication with parents requires repeated announcements of the same activity, maybe even phone calls by class parents. It is very important to make the effort. Parents are often overloaded with information and may need reminders. Sometimes parents can be opposed to positive changes, or any changes, for that matter, if they do not know about them and do not participate in the decision-making process. So, keep them informed!

HOLD CONVENIENT MEETINGS

Active participation in the PTA also involves scheduling meetings when parents can come. Agendas can be posted the day before the meeting. Experiment with having meetings in the evening and before school in the morning. Sometimes the morning meetings work better, especially in schools with before-school clubs or a breakfast program. (See calendar illustration as an example for scheduling.)

For evening meetings, have paid babysitters from the after-school program who could stay a couple of extra hours. It is important to have child care available so that parents can concentrate on the meeting and not worry about their children. More parents will attend if child care is provided.

Sustaining Your Efforts

BUILDING TEAM SPIRIT: CLEANUP DAY

One of the best ways to make parents feel part of a team is to organize activities that involve all the parents in the school. One

MAY

Lunes	Martes	Miercoles	Jueves	Viernes
Monday	**Tuesday**	**Wednesday**	**Thursday**	**Friday**
			1	**2** Principal/ Parents Chat 8:40-9:30am rm 132
5 HALF-DAY for grades K-5 12pm dismissal	**6** ESPET Test grade 4 WRITING Test grade 5	**7** PEP Reading Test grade 3	**8**	**9**
12 Parent Workshop "What You Can Do About Teasing and Bullying" 5:30-8:30pm P.S. 75	**13** ESPET Test 5/13-20 grade 4 WRITING Test grade 5	**14** PEP Math Test grade 3 Parent/Staff Retreat 3:30-8:30pm St. Michael's Church	**15**	**16**
19 School Based Planning Council Mtg. 4:15-6pm rm. 218	**20**	**21** Parent/Staff Retreat 3:30-8:30pm St. Michael's Church Jane Burak's Parent Mtg. 8:40-9:30 AM Rm:218	**22**	**23**
26 SCHOOL CLOSED MEMORIAL DAY	**27**	**28** PTA Meeting- Election of Officers for 1997-98 7pm Auditorium	**29** Parent/Staff Retreat 3:30-8:30pm St. Michael's Church CSD 3 Spanish Book Fair- P.S. 84	**30**

effective event is an All-School Classroom Cleanup Day. During this event, parents clean their children's classrooms, build shelves, shampoo rugs, and do anything else to help the teacher improve the environment in the classroom. The atmosphere is like that of an old-fashioned barnraising where the entire community or extended family gets together to build a barn. Parents get to meet each other and get to know the teacher better. The best time to hold this activity is on a Saturday in the early fall when more parents are able to attend. Holding it before school starts will work if families are back from summer vacations.

SOCIAL EVENTS FOR THE WHOLE FAMILY

Theme dances are an educational and enjoyable social activity for parents, kids, and even grandparents. Some possibilities for these dances include a Halloween Dance with everyone coming in costume, a Harvest Square Dance with Pilgrim or Western costumes, a Salsa Dance, and a Spring Planting Dance, which can have Native American and Immigrant costumes.

Another great PTA-sponsored event, which celebrates many cultures, is the International Night that was described in chapter 2. On that night children perform songs and dances, recite poems, and do short skits about various countries. After the performance, an international dinner is served in the cafeteria.

CREATE AN ANTIBIAS COMMITTEE TO INCREASE PARENT PARTICIPATION

In PS 75, as in many schools, there is a very diverse population. The PTA established the Antibias Committee to overcome biases within the parent body, using a grant from the Peace Foundation in Amherst, Massachussetts. The grant proposal was written by a parent.

Sometimes parents and teachers need a forum where they can confront the biases in our society in meaningful discussions. All the different groups in a school need to participate in the decision-making process of the Parents' Association and School Management Council. An antibias committee or similar group can help in that effort, meeting monthly to discuss concerns. All-day workshops can be held during the first year, one for parents and one for teachers, to educate the community.

One of the first issues to come up in the Antibias Committee was the lack of observance of Black History Month. International Night was not enough of a celebration for African-American families and teachers in the school. After discussing this issue at a meeting of the Antibias Committee, Grace Weiss, a parent, offered to organize a schoolwide celebration for Black History Month, involving tours to Harlem, bulletin boards celebrating famous African-American men and women, and other special events for the children and parents. This celebration has grown every year.

Another issue was a complaint by a father who felt that too much African-American history was being taught so that not enough traditional American History was being studied in his son's class. This precipitated a heated discussion at the meeting. The issue was not resolved at that time, but at least the discussion brought some resentments out into the open. It made people more aware of the situation in the school and of curriculum issues. Sometimes it is enough to air feelings that people are keeping bottled up. An Antibias Group should be a safe place to bring up problems that make people uncomfortable, and hopefully to improve the situation.

Sometimes Hispanic parents or other recent immigrants seem not to be involved. Culturally, they may be supportive at home and not feel the need to be a part of the whole group, or they may be unsure of what their role should be in school. Consequently, they may not have enough representation in the PTA. For better communication among Spanish-speaking and English-speaking groups at PS 75, a Spanish language class taught by a parent for parents was created by the Antibias Committee. The committee also came up with the idea of a Salsa Dance to celebrate Hispanic families.

SUGGESTIONS FOR AN ANTIBIAS GROUP AT YOUR SCHOOL

Remember that you are role models for the children.

Do not get involved in personal disputes with other members of the group.

Listen carefully to what other people are saying.

Try to work out compromises that will satisfy everyone.

Remember that our society is becoming more richly diverse and that discussions like this are vital to maintaining peace.

Discuss how the decisions made in the group will affect the children.

Come up with positive actions to change the social climate.

Use the Antibias Committee as another way to encourage parents to become active participants in improving the school.

SUSTAINING A WELL-RUN PARENTS' ASSOCIATION FROM YEAR TO YEAR

It is vital for the work of the PTA to continue supporting the students from year to year. If the PTA has sponsored a successful program or activity in the past, the current group of parents should be able to repeat the activity if they choose to do so. To make it easier for them, a sheet of instructions can be developed and kept in a file, a notebook, or even a computer database. It should be written by the person in charge of the activity or event and filed in the office in the PTA file cabinet. The instructions should start with a basic outline of the activity but should also include comments from the coordinator concerning what worked and what did not work for your specific school population.

Every school year has different priorities, and the PTA members may decide not to do a particular activity one year. The instructions can remain in the file or computer until they are needed. Then a new coordinator can read what is involved in an activity, saving time and energy.

Handing Over the Reins

Smooth transitions from one year to the next involve handing over the reins from one group of officers to the next. Each new PTA president brings her own style and ideas to the job. This infusion of a new personality and new skills can have a revitalizing effect. To maintain the consistency of volunteer work in the PTA, it is important that a person be elected to the job who knows firsthand what is involved because it requires a large time commitment for all officers, especially the president. The PTA can help this process by having a vice president who is not only an assistant to the president but is a trainee for the job of president the following year. In this way, the vice president learns firsthand what is really involved in the job of president. With this plan, there is always a potential president-in-training to relieve the current president of worry about who will follow him as president.

In most PTAs the maximum term for president is two years. Elections are held in May each year for the following school year. That leaves the June meeting for transition and planning—an informal meeting structure works well with each outgoing officer and committee chairperson offering ideas and advice to the new one.

PARENT VOLUNTEERS IN CLASSROOMS

Parents have been volunteering in classrooms for many years. Parents who might not be interested in coming to a PTA meeting or making phone calls can help a child learn to read, or perform a puppet show, or tell a story from their childhood.

An effective PTA which contributes life to a school needs as much participation from parents as possible. It also needs to be organized effectively for projects and fundraising to occur. While this chapter has presented some ideas for recruiting and organizing active parents, this process is a long one. Ultimately, we need to create a community of parents who care about all the children in their school. This may take a few years to establish, but it is worth the effort. Parents can also be encouraged to volunteer in the school *after* their children graduate.

5

■ ■ ■

How to Start or Improve an After-School Program

A good after-school program can enhance the educational excellence of the school, help working parents with child care, and add to the sense of the school as a community center. If your Parents' Association is considering starting an after-school program, one of the first things you need to do is to compare the use of an outside after-school provider with running your own program. With an outside provider, the day-to-day administration of the program is taken care of, but parents have less control over how it is run. If you administer your own program, you have control over as well as responsibility for everything from fees and scholarships to the daily activities of the children. If there is an outside provider available in your area such as the YMCA, invite them to a Parents' Association meeting and talk about the after-school needs of the families in the school.

Your school may already have an outside provider, but the parents may want a change. Perhaps the PTA wants to experiment with a few classes that parents have requested. Every school is different and a decision should be made according to the needs and time constraints of your population.

The after-school program at PS 75 started by the PTA began in 1992. The PTA decided to start their own program for two reasons: to offer low-cost after-school care for families who needed it, and to provide enrichment classes. The school had an outside not-for-profit provider already in place, providing full-time care to about seventy children. It did a good job at a reasonable fee, but it did not have the resources to provide subsidized slots. There were a substantial number of low-income working families who could not afford $500 a year for after-school care, much less the $1,500 yearly fee that the after-school provider was charging. No money was available for scholarships for these families, so they were unable to send their children to an after-school program at the school. The provider suggested that the Parents' Association raise funds for scholarship support, which would have meant raising $50,000 for all who needed scholarships, or using a lottery to give only a few scholarships. The provider also had a strong preference for providing care only to children who came every afternoon.

The initial discussions included many concerns about the PTA's ability to run an after-school program, since no one in the organization had ever done so. Many were concerned that a PTA after-school program might drive out the existing provider and not be able to produce a workable alternative, creating a problem for the working parents who were depending on it.

Another group of parents in the school did not need child care every day. These parents were interested in one or two afternoons of special classes in areas like sports training, science, music, ceramics, or dance. It was decided that enrichment classes would not compete with the current after-school provider since the provider did not offer them. After a few PTA meetings on the subject, a committee was formed to research other schools' after-school enrichment programs. One of the parents on the committee called the schools and community centers in the immediate area and created a chart comparing price structure, offerings, enrollment, and organizational details. It became apparent after only a few calls that fees were directly related to whether the director was a volunteer or was paid. As a result of this information, parents Daina Shobrys and Kathy Kline volunteered to run the start-up effort with the idea of eventually hiring a paid director. These women had no previous experience setting up or running an after-school program. One had worked in advertising before becoming a mother, and the other had been an independent film producer.

Of a student population of about six hundred at that time, more than 60 percent were part of the federal free school lunch program. The rest of the population could afford to pay for an after-school program, and might be interested in enriched classes run by the PTA. After talking informally to some of these parents about possible class offerings, the PTA decided to try a few classes and see if the program could pay for itself.

The enrichment class instructors were recruited by word-of-mouth. The school was lucky enough to have Barbara Beck, artist and PS 75 parent, available to teach ceramics. The school custodian renovated a large, unused storage room at the school and had it rewired. Beck designed the layout of the studio, put up shelves, and ordered the kiln, which the PTA purchased. Parent volunteers built more shelves, cleaned old tables, and varnished stools.

A sports class was offered in the school gym similar to a program in another public school run by a popular summer day camp. One of the parents offered to teach musical theater since that was her profession. Parents expressed interest in duplicating a science program already offered in a number of other schools in the area at PS 75.

All of the instructors understood that if their class did not have sufficient enrollment to cover its costs, it would be cancelled and the PTA would not owe them any money. Tuition was set at approximately $15 per afternoon for a two-hour class. The school year was divided into two terms, with tuition for each term payable before classes started. So as not to compete with the current outside provider, classes were offered for four days a week. The current provider offered five days a week of after-school care.

Besides enrichment classes the PTA wanted to provide free and low-cost after-school care to families who needed it. During discussions with the principal and the school district office, the two women who were setting up the after-school program discovered a substantial resource. The school district already provided funding for sixteen one-hour classes per week after school, known as Extended Day, from November to May. These classes were taught by the classroom teachers on various days of the week. Shobrys decided to restructure the Extended Day schedule to offer classes only on Tuesday and Thursday. There was enough funding from the district to offer two choices of classes each hour for K–2 and two choices for grades 3–5. This created two full afternoons of child care. Children could attend these classes for free if they already qualified for the federal free lunch program in school. Other children who wanted to attend these classes paid $7.50 per afternoon, half the cost of enrichment classes.

The PTA decided to combine the higher-priced enrichment offerings and lower cost Extended Day classes into one program and call it the PS 75 After-School Program. The money from enrichment classes combined with district funding subsidized the lower-cost program. Parents could choose classes based on what they could afford, or send their children for free. A few scholarships could be offered each term for enrichment classes.

There were many details to organize, including the hiring of extra adults to help with supervision. To resolve the logistical problems of getting young children from their regular classroom to after-school classes, and to accommodate more children in the program by increasing class size, the PTA hired two assistant teachers for the K–2 classes. Since the PTA was in no position to hire a paid director, and none of the parents involved could be at the school during after-school hours, one of the assistant teachers was designated to "float," help children who weren't feeling well, keep an eye on the hallways, and in general be the on-site coordinator.

It took the first full year to get the program running smoothly, but now it is an integral part of the school experience. The enrichment classes currently make a modest profit, some of which is used for improvements to school facilities, such as tennis and basketball equipment in the gym, software in the computer lab, and stools in the ceramics lab. Enrichment classes offered every semester include science, ceramics, and sports. The lower-cost classes vary each semester, depending on what the classroom teachers want to teach. Some recent class offerings have been drama, math games, chess, toy making, computers, and fairy tales. The PS 75 PTA After-School Program runs from October through the end of June four afternoons a week. The total enrollment is one-third of the school population.

The outside provider is also still in the school, serving about seventy children (the same number of children as before). Even though the PTA After-School Program pays for itself, the parent in charge is still a volunteer, although she is not the on-site coordinator. Two other volunteer parents help her with finances and registration. As an incentive, these parents receive reduced tuition for their own children to attend the program.

The following list is a guide to starting a new after-school program. The rules may sound strict, but it is necessary to put them in writing for parents before they register for the program to avoid possible misunderstandings. Also included are sample after-school class offerings, with a description of each, including the minimum and maximum number of children required for the course.

HELPFUL IDEAS FOR STARTING AN AFTER-SCHOOL PROGRAM AT YOUR SCHOOL

- Survey local after-school programs for pricing, and courses.
- It is okay to start a small program to test the waters.

- Tuition must cover the cost of teachers and insurance.
- Know the after-school needs of the parents and students in your school.
- Use a volunteer director initially to save money. Recruit instructors from parents with special skills.
- Comprehensive General Liability Insurance with a standard $1,000,000 cap in both occurrence and aggregate is not expensive and is a necessity only if your program cannot use the school's existing policy (which most schools can use).
- Survey the school body to find out what classes are wanted.
- Establish child pick-up procedures in writing.
- Have an on-site coordinator.
- Open a bank account separate from the regular PTA account.
- Apply for nonprofit status for the after-school program.
- Offer free or reduced tuition to parent program administrators.
- Use assistant teachers to escort small children to classes.
- Have emergency phone numbers for after-school hours for each child in the office.
- Have parents register their children by mail if possible.
- If you need more students, advertise your program at other schools.
- Request that parents call the coordinator, not the school office, with questions.
- If, after the first class meeting, a child dislikes the class, offer to move a child to another class, provided there is room.
- Have an absolutely clear, written understanding of compensation with teachers.
- Work out a fair plan on sharing school space and on cleaning up.
- Allow at least two years to get the program established.

Sample "Rules and Conditions," Second Term, PS 75 ASP, 1996

1. Registration form and payment are due January 19. Either mail in or drop off at the School Office (in the ASP box). If

you want to pay in cash, you may do so in the main office from 8:40 A.M. to 9:30 A.M., January 19–21.

2. Refunds are made only before the first class meeting.

3. There is a $10 charge for returned checks, with payment due immediately in cash or money order.

4. PTA After-School will not meet on K–5 half-days. Remember our outside after-school vendor runs a special program off-site on those days.

5. Security is very important. If there is someone who is not supposed to pick up your child, please notify the coordinator. The information will be shared only with those teachers who need to know.

6. If any program fills up, we will establish a waiting list.

7. Attendance will be taken. If a child has three unexcused absenses from a class, his or her place will be given to someone on the waiting list.

8. Children are expected to follow the same rules for behavior as during the regular school day. Each child is required to follow the teacher's instructions and participate in activities as directed. Children who are unable or unwilling to behave in an appropriate manner will be asked to leave the program.

   The following procedure will be used if there is an infraction of the basic rules: First, a warning will be given to the child. Second, if behavior persists, the family will be contacted to discuss the problem. Third, if there is no improvement, the child will be asked to leave the program after consultation with the principal. There are no refunds in this case.

9. All students report to the auditorium at 3 P.M. *the first week of classes only*. Assistant teachers will pick up kindergartners and escort them there. First-grade teachers will drop their kids off at the back of the first floor hallway, where an assistant teacher will be waiting to take them to the auditorium. Students will then sort themselves out into classes and go to the classroom with their after-school teachers.

10. Courses will run only if enrollment minimums are met. The PTA reserves the right to cancel offerings if numbers are not sufficient.

Dismissal time is at 5 P.M. regardless of the length of actual instruction. If arrangements are made in advance, parents may leave their children as late as 6 P.M. Any children left after 6 P.M., if their families cannot be reached, *will be taken to the local police station* at 6:15 P.M.. (Note: This must be cleared with the police first. It has never been necessary at PS 75 to take a child to the police station. It is the policy of last resort.)

Sample Course Offerings for Enrichment Classes

Ceramics and Three-Dimensional Art (Grades K–5) Mon 3 P.M. to 5 P.M. or Tues 3 P.M. to 5 P.M.

Students work in clay, glazing and firing their pieces, and explore a wide variety of other media to create very exciting objects. Minimum Enrollment: 8   Maximum: 18

Sports Etcetera (Grades K–5) Mon 3 P.M. to 5 P.M. or Thurs 3 P.M. to 5 P.M.

Mr T, an experienced physical-education teacher, runs a program that focuses on having fun, becoming fit, and learning basic skills. Classes will have the gym from 3:00 P.M. to 4:30 P.M. Minimum enrollment: 12   Maximum: 20

Science Animated (Grades K–1 and 2–5) Wed 3:30 P.M. to 4:30 P.M.

Science Development Programs, run by its originator, Sylvia Hecht, presents a course that features a different topic and expert teacher each week. This award-winning program is also offered at Fordham University as a weekend program for children, as well as at other selected elementary schools in New York City. (Please see the following schedule for recent offerings.) Minimum Enrollment: 15   Maximum 20

SCIENCE ANIMATED
Fall 1997 Schedule

ct. 8 From Flower to Fruit, Amy O'Donnell, American Museum of Natural History. Find out who assists in the amazing process from flower to fruit. An art-related activity.

ct. 15 Patterns in Nature, Angela Tripi-Weiss, Art Workshop Leader, American Museum of Natural History. Develop an artist's eye to pick out patterns in nature.

ct. 22 Going Batty!, Susan Rolon, New York Aquarium. Explore the many faces of bats. Make a bat mask.

ct. 29 How-To/Can-Do Science, Ted Arin, Manhattan Community College. Introducing the magical world of chemistry using household materials. A surprise treat.

ov. 5 Clothing = Climate = Culture, Kevin Orangers, American Museum of Natural History. Symbolisms & uses of clothing in Western Africa & South America. Make something to make & wear.

ov. 12 World of Mini-Mammals, Kathleen Lamattina, Bronx Wildlife Center. The habits & habitats of small mammals, i.e., a ferret, mink, hedgehog, rabbit & more. Live specimens.

ov. 19 Tales of Whales, Leann Gast, New York Aquarium. Sound tracks, movies, artifacts to handle, & a project to make & take.

ov. 26 It's a Dog's Life, Jean Augustin, American Museum of Natural History. With special signals, rewards & love, a dog can become a much-valued best friend.

ec. 3 Paper Transformations, Gay Merrill Gross, Member, Origami, U.S.A. It's a bird! It's a boat! It's a whale! What will this peice of paper become?

ec. 10 The Story of Money, Lisa Breslof, American Museum of Natural History. Learn how money began and how it was made. Examine currency & detect counterfeits.

ec. 17 The Jewelry from the Earth, Amy O'Donnell, American Museum of Natural History. Design your own adornments with natural materials such as clay, shells, seeds & more as cultures do all around the world.

an. 7 Touch & Tell, Jean Augustin, American Museum of Natural History. Learn by using only the sense of touch, without looking, to experience the natural sciences.

an. 14 Tee Shirt Tech, Janet Zukowski, Parsons School of Design. How to use natural & regular dyes to color & make designs on fabric. **BRING a new white T-shirt & a plastic hanger.**

an. 22 Hidden Animals in the "Big Apple," Frank Indiviglio, Bronx Wildlife Center. Observe a variety of live, wild creatures, which, unknown to most people, live in the heart of the City.

an. 29 The Sound of Music, Ken Koga-Moriuchi, Science Consultant. Experiments with physics of sound. Class will make & play a variety of unusual musical instruments.

6
∎ ∎ ∎

Fund-Raising Ideas

Bake sales, spaghetti suppers, and pancake breakfasts are traditional fund-raising activities in public schools. These social events encourage families to participate in school activities, while raising money at the same time. Unfortunately, dinners and breakfasts don't raise enough money to cover an ever-expanding PTA budget.

Politicians continually promise more money for education, but despite their promises, fund-raising by parents is still essential. Sophisticated methods are necessary to raise enough money to enrich, expand, and sadly, in some schools, to provide even a basic education, a roof repair, or a new playground. Some schools are lucky to have parents who have the means to give time or money to the school. Other schools do not have a population that can afford to spend a lot of time or money on the school. Fund-raising, like other forms of volunteerism, must fit into the schedules of the people who make it happen as well as the culture of the school itself.

Parent groups must choose which types of fund-raisers they want to concentrate on. These choices are based on such factors as: the time of year, the income level of the school population, and the amount of money that is needed. The following questionaire is useful for parent organizations when they are deciding what fund-raisers to put on in any given year. These questions will help the PTA make appropriate choices and can prove invaluable to the success or failure of overall fund-raising for the year.

1. How much money does the school need to raise this year?
2. How many volunteers are available and what kind of help can they provide?
3. What kinds of fund-raisers have been successful in the past at the school?
4. How many fund-raisers can the school realistically support in one year?
5. Should there be many little fund-raisers or one large one for this school year?
6. What is the best time of year to schedule each fund-raiser?
7. Are there enough people willing to be in charge of each event?
8. Are the parents willing to experiment with a new type of fund-raiser or do they prefer sticking with known successful methods?
9. Does the school want to involve the outside community in raising money for the school?
10. Is there a committee for writing grant proposals?

This overview will not cover every type of fund-raiser, but it will examine a variety of large and small fund-raising ideas. Each idea is discussed in terms of potential earnings, how many people are needed, and how long it will take to plan and complete. Every idea in this chapter has proved to be successful for schools, whether done on a large or small scale.

Grant proposals are an alternative to fund-raising events. We will discuss grants as a source of funding with Susan Woolhandler, a public school parent and a professional fund-raiser and author. Her simple guide is useful for novice proposal writers. Gil Turchin, a financial expert with extensive experience in obtaining grants for School District 3 in New York City, also shares helpful information on sources for grants and what to include in every grant proposal.

EASY-TO-ORGANIZE FUND-RAISERS

Gift Wrap and Holiday Candy Sales

Many schools across the country sell gift wrap as their main annual fund-raiser. They do this fund-raiser because this type of sale earns a lot of money for the time spent, and usually involves a majority of the families in the school.

The best wrapping paper distributors make it easy to organize the sale. They should supply all promotional announcements, wrap and label each family's order individually, box deliveries for each teacher's class separately, and deliver orders directly to the school. They often offer advice on how to keep track of the money turned in, although parents are responsible for collecting it and depositing it in a bank account. These companies frequently pay the school 50 percent of the retail price. This can add up to quite a lot of money if most of the school families participate. For an average school of 600 students, the usual profit is $12,000 to $15,000, while $20,000 or more is not unheard of in schools with almost 100% participation from families. The larger the school, of course, the larger the profit potential.

Parents can sell on their own time to fellow workers at the office, or to neighbors and relatives. This has the added advantage of bringing in money from people beyond the parent body. An early fall sale is timed perfectly for gift giving around the holidays, and many of the companies offer boxed candy as well as wrapping paper.

A small group of only five or six parents and a coordinator are needed to organize the sale. A few of the parent volunteers check the orders when they are turned in and count the money. The parent coordinator and two or three parents are needed on-site to manage delivery to the classes.

The parent coordinating the sale should compare carefully what these companies offer before working with them. Some charge up to 3 percent for prizes the children receive for selling different amounts of merchandise. The prizes offered by these companies, ranging from such things as stuffed animals to bicycles, can effectively motivate children to sell more merchandise. The amount sold can be greater because of these prizes, but the cost of the prizes does come out of the 50% profit the school earns.

Money can be saved if parents think of alternate ways to reward the children; class pizza parties or ice-cream parties for the classes who sell the most are effective. Movie or sports tickets are excellent rewards for the high sellers. The school can also order its own prizes from a mail-order catalog and offer bicycles or other large items as top prizes. The prizes purchased by the Parents' Association or donated by local merchants are more cost-effective than the ones the company provides.

Many school districts have chosen to limit the number of major direct-sales campaigns involving the children to one or two per year. This limitation actually makes the one or two sales more effective, because a greater number of parents and students participate in each sale. If there are too many direct-sales campaigns in the school year, it can be overwhelming for the children and the community.

Some school districts only permit sales in which the school's profit is 50 percent of the sales price. Parents need to check the policy on fund-raising with their local school district before beginning a large direct-sales fund-raiser.

A warning to all families because of recent tragedies involving children who have been harmed when selling door-to-door in their own neighborhoods. *Never allow your child to sell items door-to-door without being accompanied by a parent or adult friend.*

Chocolate Bar Sales

Chocolate candy bars are an ever-popular school fund-raiser. Bands, choruses, and senior classes frequently sell them to pay for trips. Some schools do not sell them because they don't want to encourage the children to eat candy. Many parents, however, find candy easier to sell at work than expensive gift wrap. It is an impulse item that can be sold many times to the same people. Profit margins are usually 50 percent. Candy can be sold at any time of the year to make up a budget shortfall in the Parents Association or to pay for a special event.

The hardest part of a candy sale is finding a workable way to collect the money. It is easier to collect the money when the boxes of bars are distributed, though this may discourage some people from selling. Since the bars are sold for cash, the collection of money needs to be carefully monitored, either with a sign-out system making the parents responsible, or payment in advance from each family.

Magazine Sales

Many schools sell magazine subscriptions to raise money. Magazine sales are similar to gift wrap and candy sales in that parents and students approach friends and relatives. Though it is a similar type of selling, in some ways magazines are easier to sell than wrapping paper. There is nothing to deliver, and people can simply extend subscriptions to magazines that they currently receive, as well as subscribe to a new magazine. Friends and relatives can subscribe from anywhere in the country if the forms are sent to them by mail.

There is no mark-up on the subscription price, unlike the wrapping paper, which is sold at a premium. The schools typically receive as much as 40 percent of the subscription price. Some of the magazine distributors also offer books, cassettes, CDs, and computer software. Prize programs are also available for magazine sales. As with the gift wrap, the prizes must be paid for out of the profits, and more money will be made if the school designs its own reward program.

Magazine sales require even fewer parents than a gift wrap sale because volunteers are only needed to hand out the instruction packets supplied by the magazine distributor. The money is turned in to the office by individual parents and collected later, from the office, by a parent coordinator. These packets have everything needed to participate, including a goal-setting sign for the lobby of the school, showing how many more subscriptions are needed to meet the goal. While magazine subscriptions can be credited to the school at any time during the year in most of these programs, the most successful drives last about two to three weeks. See the end of the chapter for a list of gift wrap and magazine distributors.

Supermarket Cash Cards

Some supermarket chains around the country have started to give a 1–3 percent cash rebate to local public schools. This is a great idea whose time has come. Because of computerized checkout systems in the stores, it is easy for them to keep track of how much credit goes to each school, based on the amount purchased. The parents show a cash card to the checkout clerk, who reads it into the computer at the time of purchase. The card has a code for the school on it. The supermarket then sends a check to the school each quarter, or when parents' purchases reach a few thousand dollars, depending on the program.

The more times parents, grandparents, or other relatives shop for food and show their card, the more money the school makes. This is a successful partnership for both the schools and the supermarkets, who get a lot of very loyal customers. It requires almost no effort from the parents once it is set up, since they have to buy groceries anyway. The school reminds parents periodically to bring their cards to the supermarket and show them to the cashier.

Some schools receive as much as $10,000 to $20,000 each year with regular parent participation. Check with the local school district to find out if supermarkets in your area participate already, or call a store and persuade them to start a new program. When parent Barbara Pace was PTA president at Dry Ridge Elementary in Kentucky, she set up a new rebate program at the IGA supermarket in her area by going to her local store and working with them directly.

Some supermarkets in different parts of the country that currently have cash rebate programs include: Kroger, Publix, IGA, Safeway, Giant and Foodland (in Hawaii).

Capital Fund Drives by Mail

This is a low-level organizational effort that can produce a lot of money, depending on the parent body. The PTA president or the head of fund-raising makes a written appeal to all families. The appeal outlines why the money is needed and what it will be used for specifically once it is raised. Charities and other nonprofit organizations have used this method of fund-raising for many years. Parents and relatives can be very receptive to this approach, especially if the letter outlines exactly how the money will be used in the school. This type of fund-raiser is the easiest of all with just a letter to be written, copied, and mailed to the entire parent body.

Neighbors and merchants can also be put on the mailing list. Many people like to support the public schools even though they do not have children currently enrolled. Schools with a 501(c) 3 designation (official nonprofit status) can offer tax deductions for contributors.

This direct-appeal campaign has been successful at many schools around the country. At Beverly Farms Elementary and at PS 75 contributors have donated thousands of dollars in a single year for specific needs, such as new computers for a lab. An example of a pledge letter is included at the end of this chapter, as is information on the IRS publication for information about nonprofit status.

Know your school's population. This direct appeal will not work in all schools, especially in some low-income urban or rural schools. If the school has a low-income population, people do not have any extra money to give. These schools are better served if parents aggressively solicit federal, state, and corporate grants to make up any deficits in school programs. See the end of this chapter for a list of corporations who have given money to schools.

School districts, principals, and parents can work together with federal and state agencies to make fund allocation as equitable as possible. In the state of Kentucky, equitable distribution of funds has been mandated by law to help schools in lower-income areas. The program spreads state funding around by awarding large cash payments to schools with high test scores in a broad range of academic areas; the tests are administered in fourth and fifth grades. This system rewards successful schools, whether rich or poor, and is being used as a model for other parts of the country.

School Photos

School photos are an area that may be overlooked as a fund-raiser. Money can be made from school photos, especially as class and individual pictures are going to be taken every year anyway.

When choosing a school photographer, the parent coordinator in charge must compare pricing structures and negotiate the best deal for the school. Some charge a flat fee and allow the school to mark up the price according to what the school population can afford. Others take a percentage depending on how many photos are purchased. For an average school of 600 students, a profit of $2,000 to $4,000 is possible, depending on the percentage agreed upon with the photographer.

Parents buy more pictures if they have proofs to choose from, rather than paying in advance and being stuck with the pose the photographer chooses. Another advantage of proofs is that every child is photographed without having to remember to bring in money first. More parents buy when they see the photo in their hands. However, the proof system makes more work for the photo coordinator, since it creates more stages: Proofs go home first, parents turn in their choices with payment, and then final packages have to be distributed. Each time they are sent home or back to school, or sent to the lab, the coordinator has to sort them and take action. It does not involve many parents, only a very small committee of three or four people.

Some schools also offer family portraits as an additional fundraiser. Each family portrait earns a higher percentage than individual student pictures. Parents buy a sitting in advance so the school can be assured of meeting a minimum number of sittings required by the photographer.

Bake Sales at Election Polls and School Events

Bake sales are the most traditional way for parents to make money for schools. A simple bake sale for which parents make homemade goodies to sell is still effective and fun. Many different types of bake sales can be offered for many different purposes, from a concession stand at special school events to a sale for an individual class.

Many schools organize a large bake sale near the polling area on an election day, when neighbors come in to vote. The PS 75 PTA earned $5000 with a bake sale during the presidential election of 1992. At that election, voter turnout was especially high, and parents baked lots of goodies and worked very hard on the day of the sale. Some pies and cakes were sold whole, and many bagels and muffins were snapped up by voters on the way to work. PTA workers brought coffee to voters as they waited in line to vote.

Election-day bake sales require an early start. Someone must get to school and start brewing the coffee. Large coffee urns can sometimes take half an hour to make coffee. When the polls open at 6:00 A.M., food and coffee should be available for the early-bird voters.

If school is closed on election day, children can help sell with their parents, making it more fun for everyone. Families can drop off items the day before if there is a good place to store them. More things can be brought in on the sale day itself. Volunteers are needed to sell in one- or two-hour shifts while the polls are open, with the greatest number of people needed before and after work. Since everything is donated, profits are high. Preplanning involves signing up volunteers to bake, bring, and sell.

LARGE EVENTS REQUIRING MORE ORGANIZATIONAL EFFORT

Festivals, Carnivals and Fairs

A festival, carnival, or fair can be a very rewarding event for everyone involved, including both the school and the community. This can be a small event, simple to plan and just for fun, or a large enterprise requiring a lot of planning, which can bring in enough money for the entire PTA budget for the year. Some urban schools put on large annual street fairs. These fairs raise money by renting booth space to outside vendors for selling their wares. The people in the booths sell all sorts of things: food, handmade crafts, clothing, tools, and other merchandise.

Sometimes school groups rent a large inflated bouncing castle for children to play in, which is usually worth the rental fees, since it can be seen from far away and will attract more people to the street fair. The rental fees can run as high as $350 a day, and so this should be used only if good weather and a large turnout of kids is expected. Other means of attracting people include pony rides, rented amusement rides, bagpipers, petting zoos, and local television, radio, or sports personalities signing autographs.

Street fairs need to be publicized to be very successful and they require extensive preplanning. Effective methods include advertising in local papers, community announcements on radio, and street banners announcing the event in advance.

Carnivals have of a variety of games for the kids. Ring toss, toothpick sculptures, sand art, spin art, Hit the Basket, face painting, cupcake decorating, and fishing for treasures are a few of the favorites. Each class in the school can create an activity or game, and parents take turns supervising. A carnival will fit inside the school during bad weather or winter months. Food is sold and everyone has a lot of fun, especially the children.

Although money can be made from such an event, it doesn't have the potential earnings of a large street fair or community festival, unless outside vendors are allowed to rent booth space. Profits range from $500 to $5000 or more for a large, well-organized, and well-attended carnival.

Auctions and Silent Auctions

Auctions are very labor-intensive but rewarding events. The type that private schools have traditionally held can raise anywhere from $5,000 to $150,000, but they require much planning and many volunteers. Auctions are also social events for parents and friends, who get dressed up, pay to feast on food donated by local restaurants, and bid on donated items, raising thousands of dollars for the school.

It takes a very organized and optimistic auction coordinator to make an auction successful, someone who can motivate parents and create an overall plan of action with target dates. At PS 75 the PTA was fortunate to have Lisa Alonge Greenfield as the coordinator for the first two auctions held at the school. She and her steering committee were so enthusiastic, organized, and energetic that both auctions were tremendously successful, each earning about $28,000 for the school. Current coordinator Kate Maitland has also been very successful.

Materials from the second auction held at PS 75 in the fall of 1996 are included at the end of the chapter. The auction newsletter and catalog illustrate some of the many facets of putting on such an event. It may look like an overwhelming task, but it gets easier after the first year, since the procedures are set and information is stored in computer databases.

Auction newsletters keep parents informed and excited about the upcoming event during the weeks of preparation required. They give people ideas for things to donate, businesses to contact, or ways to contribute. Many parents are needed to solicit donations from local merchants, by phone and in person. Each donor signs a form with three copies, authorizing the school to offer the item at the auction. Each donor keeps a copy so that when the purchaser comes to collect, the merchant has a record of the agreement with the school.

The school should be able to store items that parents have collected or donated for the auction unless alternate arrangements can be made. On the day before and the day of the auction, volunteers are needed to set up the school gymnasium (or other location) selected for the dinner and the silent auction items to be displayed. Rented chairs, tables, donated flowers, and tablecloths (on loan from hotels, restaurants, or families) must be set up. If possible, arrange to have access to credit-card purchasing for the evening. Call the credit-card companies to arrange this convenience. When purchasers are able to use a credit card, sales increase.

An auction is a reflection of the school community that creates it. No two are exactly alike. Having items made by the children themselves is a good idea. Parent-sewn quilts constructed from squares of cloth with children's drawings or handprints on them are very popular. Child-painted furniture, such as small tables or chairs, or painted shower curtains are always a big hit. It is a good idea to have items available for sale at all price ranges to encourage everyone to participate. A table with items for $10 or less encourages participation by people who may not want to buy higher-priced items. A fine dinner for the price of admission ($5 to $20) with donated food from a restaurant or market is a great way for everyone to be included even if they don't buy anything at the auction.

Examples from the PS 75 auction catalog show other types of things that can be offered. Combination packages of donations are popular, such as: dinner at a specific restaurant with two tickets to a show or sports event. Weekends at families' vacation homes make great auction items. The homemade gourmet dessert of the month—or brunch for 12 people—made or brought to your home on the weekend of your choice, are other big hits.

A live auctioneer generates humor and excitement. This not only earns more money for the school, but it makes the event more fun for everyone and should be worth the fee. With advance publicity, people will start to look forward to the evening and will invite friends, especially if they know they can have a good time and help a good cause at the same time.

Year-Round Flea Market

The story of this flea market is included because it is a true story of parents recognizing an opportunity in their community and acting on it for the benefit of public schools. This type of weekly flea market can be established in any town or city with cooperation from the community and the schools.

On the Upper West Side in New York City there is a year-round Sunday flea market in the yard of Intermediate School 44. From its grassroots beginning, it has blossomed into Greenflea Market, a 501(c)3 nonprofit corporation. This market has successfully served the needs of public school children in School District 3 for over fifteen years, providing after-school programs, supplies, and other necessities. It operates rain or shine every week.

In the early 1980s, local vendors had been informally using the school yard on weekends to sell their wares. Parents at the school, seeing a fund-raising opportunity, approached them about formalizing the arrangement. The parents realized that a regular flea market could benefit both the two schools nearby as well as the vendors themselves.

The Parents' Associations of the two schools near the yard, PS 87 and IS 44, and the New York City Council on the Environment, founded the Greenflea Corporation in 1985. The Board of Education leases the lot to Greenflea, which pays a large portion of its gross revenue to District 3. Since its incorporation, Greenflea has earned more than $1,000,000 in profit for the schools in the district. Greenflea is still run by a volunteer board of directors, responsible for its long survival. The board makes all decisions for the program, including how the funds earned by Greenflea will be spent at the schools. The funding priorities change every year and may include such things as books, art supplies, computers, a librarian's salary, or a dance program. Students pay only a nominal fee every year to participate in the after-school program at IS 44, which Greenflea underwrites.

The vendors rent spaces to sell a colorful collection of items, both old and new. Over half the items sold are new, and it is always a treasure hunt for shoppers, since the vendors' merchandise is so varied. Rugs, antiques, plants, food, books, toys, clothing, crafts, jewelry, furniture, housewares, and fresh produce are some of the many items offered for sale.

In the early stages of the market, it was run entirely by volunteers, but sometimes the volunteers couldn't be there on Sundays to help out. To have more reliable workers, the organization hired a full-time, paid administrator and currently employs seventeen people who perform security, site preparation, and clean-up jobs.

This flea market is successful partly because of its central location, on a popular shopping avenue near a museum. It could work well in many areas of the country, but it should have a good location, good publicity (signs, ads, and word of mouth), and be easily visible and accessible to shoppers. If set up as a nonprofit corporation working in partnership with a volunteer board from the schools, it can be a great on-going community project creating substantial financial support for local schools. If it becomes an institution like Greenflea, the parents who started it can be proud of their contribution to the schools for many years to come.

If you would like more information about how to start a profitable market like Greenflea, contact: Community School District 3 Office (in New York City), 300 West 96th Street, New York, New York 10025.

OBTAINING GRANTS FOR YOUR SCHOOL

Many grants are available for schools. These can be from federal, state, and city agencies and a variety of other sources. Having a small committee on the PTA to research and write proposals for grants can be a steady source for funds to enrich your school's programs.

Gil Turchin is an Assistant Superintendent at District 3 in New York City. He is the resident expert on grant writing and resources for all schools in the district. I spoke with him in the district office where we discussed how he sees future funding for schools. In our discussions he pointed out that there are changes in fund-raising of which parents in schools may not be aware.

Historically, large scale fund-raising has been done at the district level and has been distributed to schools based on need. Examples of federal funding include allocative programs such as Title I (poverty), PCEN (low achievement), and LEP AID (25 percent having limited English-proficiency). How these funds are used in the school has been controlled by the government agency providing the money. Parents usually do not have a voice in how the funds are allocated in the school.

The laws governing use of these funds are changing. In New York and many other states, by the year 2000, allocative and tax levy money will be given directly to individual schools. Parents will be able, through school management councils, to make decisions on how to spend the money once it comes to the school.

Goals 2000, a half-billion dollar federal program, awards money to individual schools based on their Comprehensive Education Plan. Every school will have a plan designed by the school council with help from their district office. This is good news for the schools with strong school management councils who are ready and able to allocate the money within the school.

Other sources of funds exist besides government grants. Gil points out that parents can find money for their school by doing a little research on competitively funded grant programs. He outlined three types of sources to explore.

Grants from Neighborhood Businesses

Awards can vary from $500 to $2,500. Many businesses will give money to schools. Banks, especially where the school has an account, are a good source of money. See the branch manager for guidelines. The local office of the gas and electric company sometimes gives grants to schools, and the telephone company is another potential source.

Business or fraternal organizations include the Chamber of Commerce, Kiwanis, Lions, Rotary, and others. If you are new to grant writing, ask for help from your school district office. Keep in mind that the school is in competition with all other neighborhood groups for this grant money, so it pays to apply to as many sources as possible.

Corporate Support

Corporations will often give grants of $10,000 or more. Make a list of corporations in the area of the school by walking or driving around the immediate area of the school or using the telephone book. Write to the directors of corporate support and ask for a copy of their contribution policies and programs, and a list of whom they gave to last year. Find out their local and national policy on supporting schools. Also ask for an annual report, and study their goals and philosophy statement.

Any request for money should use language that reflects the philosophy and goals of that particular corporation. Requests for money should also support, if possible, the area of expertise for the corporation, such as media for Time-Warner or computer software for Microsoft. Also survey the parent body to find out if any of them are employees of corporations with matching grant programs. (See "Information Sheet for Parents Soliciting Donations of Goods and Services From Corporations," at the end of this chapter.)

Ask for What You Need

A parent at PS 75 obtained three convection ovens for classroom cooking projects directly from the manufacturer simply by calling and asking them to give the ovens to the school. If you have the nerve, this direct approach can be a very easy and effective way to obtain whatever your school may need. The nonprofit status of 501(c)3 can encourage corporations to donate new or used items. Items such as paper supplies, computers, tables, art supplies, musical instruments, tape or audio equipment, VCRs, and countless others can be obtained from corporations by asking for them.

Foundations

For foundations, go to the local library and look for the local Regional Foundation Directory (there are 200 such directories for different areas of the country). Or visit their website on the Internet. Many of the same steps used for corporations are used for foundations. Ask for an annual report and for a set of guidelines and applications for submitting grant proposals. Look at the areas of interest of the foundation. Find out from the annual report what kinds of programs they fund. Look at the list of the board of directors, and circulate this list among your committee members to locate possible personal contacts. This is a very important step in securing foundation support.

Complaining about how bad things are for your school doesn't carry as much weight as it once did. Language such as "We are the poorest..." is not compelling. Instead be positive. Present your vision and what you will do to make your vision a reality. Most "cold" solicitation proposals are two to three pages long, unless there are specific guidelines.

Gil Turchin has been very successful in the past few years at obtaining grants for District 3. He helped secure a large three-year National Science Foundation grant to improve the level of science instruction in the schools. He secured an eight-million-dollar, two-year grant from NYNEX called the Diffusion Fund Grant. This grant was so large that Districts 3, 5, 12, 18, and 30 combined forces to work on it together. It supplies the technology for interactive distance learning, a very exciting use of video teleconferencing. See chapter 7 for a more detailed description. Every school district in the country should find someone like Gil Turchin to secure funding successfully.

Gil Turchin's Essentials for Writing a Successful Proposal

Needs Assessment: Details the problem
Goals and Objectives: What should happen in spite of problems?
Activities: What will be implemented with the money?
Evaluation of the program: How will it be judged a success?
Personnel: How many are needed to run the program?
Budget: How much money will be needed in each area?

Susan Woolhandler is a second grade parent at PS 75 in New York City; she is also an author and a professional fund-raiser and grant-proposal writer. She and a small number of other grant-writing parents at that school have been very successful in obtaining grants that have increased the educational offerings.

Susan's Woolhandler's Hints to Parents for Obtaining Grants

Get it turned in on time; missed deadlines are disqualifying.
Answer all questions; don't leave blanks.
Give them what they ask for. If they ask for three goals, don't give

them two, even if well-written, because they may just throw it out.

Don't write too much; this should not be the "great American novel." Fewer, but concrete, examples are better.

Don't forget to include a description of how the program will be evaluated.

Include a budget with realistic estimates.

Buzzwords such as "parental engagement" instead of "parental involvement" may carry more weight. Ask advice from school district experts on any special language to use.

For first attempts, adopt a successful "model" from another school and make yours similar to it.

If your school has gotten grants before, read over successful proposals to see if any sections can be reused.

Form alliances with teachers to find out what type of grant they want and how they would use it in the classroom.

Deadlines

Federal agencies start preparing grant options for schools in September. They complete and send Requests for Proposals out to schools or districts by December 31. Deadlines are frequently at the end of February. By the end of April, schools receiving the grants are notified of awards to be used for the following school year. The person or committee writing the proposal typically has about six weeks in which to complete and turn in the application.

There are two kinds of federal grants. The first is a large grant designed to be shared with 80 percent of the schools that apply. The second is a grant, large or small, awarded to only a few schools. If the grant is in the first group, you have very little to lose by applying, since the chances are good that your school will be funded. If it is in the second group, you might think twice before applying unless you have a very special idea or a school population that is tailor-made for the grant.

Advantages of Having Official Nonprofit Status

If your school's parent group has a member who is either a lawyer or an accountant willing to do the paperwork, see if he or she will, without charge, apply for official nonprofit status, 501(c)3. This can increase charitable donations to the school. When parents solicit matching corporate employee grants or any kind of corporate donation, the company usually wants to know if the school has nonprofit status.

A 501(c)3 designation is for the Internal Revenue Service, but it also entitles the group to apply to the state for sales-tax exemption. It may increase the amount of paperwork the treasurer does each year, but it is certainly worthwhile if the school gets more donations as a result. For more information about nonprofit status with the IRS, call the IRS customer service line at 1-800-829-3676 and ask for IRS Publication # 557.

For More Information on Fund-Raising

An important book for schools interested in fund-raising is *Raising Funds for Your Child's School*, by Cynthia Francis Gensheimer (published by Walker and Company, New York). This definitive book on fund-raising in schools was written by a parent. The book contains detailed instructions, including time lines and follow-up for over sixty different ideas. Based on what actually works in real schools all over the country, it includes addresses to contact for all merchandise mentioned in the book.

Resources

A partial listing of companies that give to public elementary schools follows (from the Corporate Giving Directory, 1998 TAFT). Contact these companies for guidelines.

Alliant Techsystems, AlliedSignal Inc., Allstate Insurance Co., Andersen Corp., ARCO Chemical Co., Bandag, Inc., Bankers

Trust Co., Bean, Inc., L.L., Bechtel Group, Inc., Boston Edison Co., Burlington Industries, Inc., Burlington Resources, Inc., Clorox Co., Consolidated Natural Gas Co., Cray Research, Inc., General Mills, Inc., Hasbro, Inc., Hewlett-Packard Co., Honeywell, Inc., Hughes Electronics Corporation, The Prudential Insurance Co., of America, Public Service Electric & Gas Co., The Reader's Digest Association, Inc., Red Wing Shoe Co., Inc., Reynolds Metals Co., RJR Nabisco Inc., Rockwell International Corporation., Royal Insurance, Rubbermaid Inc., Ryder System, Inc., SAFECO Corp., Saint Paul Companies, Inc., Salomon, Inc., SBC Communications, Inc., Schlumberger Ltd., Charles Schwab & Co., Joseph E. Seagrams & Sons, Inc., Sega of America Inc., Shell Oil Co., Shoney's Inc., Simpson Investment Co., Sonoco Products Co., Sony Electronics Inc., Southern California Gas Co., Southwest Gas Corporation., Sprint Corp., Standard Products Co., State Street Bank & Trust Co., Stelcase, Inc., Stonecutter Mills Corp., Stride Rite Corp., Sumitomo Bank of California, Sun Co., Inc., Sun Microsystems, Inc., SunTrust Co. Bank Atlanta, Tandy Corp., Tektronix, Inc., Tenneco Inc., Texaco Inc., Thomasville Furniture Industries, The Times Mirror Co., Toshiba America, Inc., Toyota Motor Sales USA, Inc., Transco Energy Co., Travelers Group, True Oil Co., TRW Inc., Unilever United States, Inc., Union Camp Corp., Union Carbide Corp., Union Electric Co., United Airlines, Inc., United States Sugar Corp., United States Trust Co., of New York, United Technologies Corp, Universal Leaf Tobacco Co., Inc., Unocal Corp., UNUM Corp., USX Corp., Varian Associates, Wachovia Bank of North Carolina, NA, Waffle House, Inc., Wal-Mart Stores, Inc., Washington Mutual Bank, Washington Post Co., Washington Water Power Co., Waste Management, Inc., Wells Fargo & Co., Westinghouse Electric Corp., Weyerhaeuser Co., Whirlpool Corp., WICOR, Inc., Wisconsin Energy Corp., Wisconsin Public Service Corp., Zachry Co., H.B.

COMPANIES THAT SELL MAGAZINES AND GIFT WRAP

QSP [a division of Reader's Digest], P.O. Box 10203, Des Moines, Iowa 50336; 1-800-678-2673.

Innisbrook Wraps, P.O. Box 16046, Greensboro, N.C. 27416; 1-800-334-8461

Sally Foster Giftwrap, P.O. Box 1868, Spartanburg, S.C. 29304; 1-800-237-9727

Genevieve's Giftwrap Sales, P.O. Box 147, W. Springfield, Mass.; 01090; 1-800-842-6656

INFORMATION SHEET FOR PARENTS SOLICITING DONATIONS OF GOODS AND SERVICES FROM CORPORATIONS

HERE ARE STEP-BY-STEP DIRECTIONS FOR SUCCESSFUL SOLICITATION OF ITEMS FROM LARGE BUSINESSES:

1. Obtain the **phone number** of the business (and write it on the information sheet so we never have to do it again!!)

2. Call the business and ask for the name and specific address of the person handling **corporate donations.** You could also get this person's specific phone number at this time. Record this as well on the information sheet.

3. Print a corporate donation letter made up specifically for this business (feel free to add any personal touches relevant to this business's interests). Ask for more than one of everything if appropriate--for example, 5 single nights at a hotel, 5 dinners for 2 or 2 dinners for 4 at a restaurant. ALWAYS PRINT LETTERS ON PS 75 LETTERHEAD!!

4. Enclose a copy of the **press release,** as well as several blank **auction donation forms,** with your **cover letter.**

5. **Mail** your request. We are asking each of you to donate the postage for the cause.

6. Follow up the mailing WITHIN 10 DAYS with a **phone call** to the contact person at the business. THIS IS ESSENTIAL TO THE PROCESS!! Ask if the person received the letter and if they can pledge something right now. If they prefer to make the actual donation after 12/31 due to their fiscal schedule, that's fine.

7. Once the donation is secured, remind them to **mail back the donation forms** as soon as possible. If they are not interested in donating this year, ask if they would like to be contacted the following year. If they say no, please note that on the info sheet.

8. **RETAIN YOUR INFORMATION SHEETS!!!** GIVE THEM TO MARION OR KAREN AT NEXT MEETING.

THANK YOU FOR YOUR HELP!!!

[Date]

[ABC Corporation]
[123 Any Street]
New York, NY 10099]

RE: PS 75's Third Annual Auction

Dear [name of contact at corporation/theater/restaurant/hotel/etc]

We are writing to ask for [ITEM] as a donation for our Third Annual Fundraising Auction.

PS 75 is a public elementary school on the Upper West Side of Manhattan. We are blessed with wonderful teachers, a dynamic principal, and about 750 enthusiastically involved families of every conceivable ethnic, educational, and socioeconomic description. And we are doing well. To judge by descriptions of our school in the New York press, we are in a state of perpetual middle-class revival!

But these are financially perilous times for the New York City public schools. That's why we need YOUR help! Our PTA must raise money every year to provide equipment and teachers for art and special reading programs. With budgets cuts at every turn and more around the corner, our fundraising efforts are truly critical.

We are in the planning stages now for this year's auction. We hope to exceed our first and second auctions' net by raising $45,000! Profits from the first annual auction helped us purchase a gleaming new computer lab. The money we raise this year will go toward theater, music, and fine art enrichment programs, and much more (perhaps some desperately needed new plumbing for the children's bathrooms???).

We are soliciting donations of goods and services from neighborhood merchants, parents, teachers, and other friends of PS 75. AND NOW IT'S YOUR TURN! The auction is scheduled for the evening of Friday, March 27, 1998. As a donor, you will be listed in our lovely auction catalogue, and you will be publicly thanked on auction night for your generousity.

Help us keep our public school community strong and viable! Thank you for your consideration.

Sincerely,

[YOUR NAME]
PS 75 parent

Table of Contents/Auction Program

Program

7:00 - 9:00	Viewing of Live Auction Items Silent Auction Buffet Dinner
9:00	Silent Auction Ends A short musical presentation begins in the auditorium
9:30 - 10:30	Live Auction (Auction may run longer if necessary)
10:30	Announcement of highest Silent Auction bidders Pay for items purchased Dessert and Coffee

❁*❀*❁*❀*❁*❀*❁*❀*❁*❀*❁*❀*❁*❀*❁*❀*❁*❀*❁*❀*❁*❀*❁*❀*❁*❀*❁*❀*❁

The Silent Auction will open at 7:00 PM and close at approximately 8:45 PM. Hundreds of goods and services will be on display. Each package or item in the Silent Auction will have a nearby sheet describing the item(s), the minimum bid and the minimum raise (usually $5). To bid on an item, enter your assigned bidder ID and your bid amount on the form next to the items of your choice. Additional bids may be added until the silent auction is officially closed. The person who entered the highest bid will win. Winners will be announced during dessert and coffee.

TIPS:

- Be prepared to keep track of the bidding on your selections. You may have to enter new bids several times to ensure a better chance of winning.

- Sharing packages with friends is economical and fun. For example, two couples can split the cost on a dinner and show for four. Or, two people can split the package that includes four facials.

- Mark the items in your catalogue that interest you before the night of the Auction. Your shopping will be easier.

☐ *1. Sweet Dreams*   **Minimum Bid $75**   **Value $250**

A solution to the small-kid's-room problem: a Bislet solid pine high bed from Ikea, good as new, with mattress, guardrail and ladder. It's 39¾" high, 78¾" long and 35 " deep. It cost $420 new; buy it and you won't have to look at Newark Airport. We'll throw in a child's book ($20) and a troll doll ($9).

☐ *2. Heart-Shaped Bed*   *$100*   *$260*

You've heard all about those wild and crazy Pocono hotels, now try any one of their four resorts. Here's a two-day, one-night weekday stay, complete with breakfast, dinner, entertainment, and full use of the facilities, at any of Caesar's Pocono resorts ($225). Preserve the memories in a photo album ($20) and take along a champagne gift basket ($15).

☐ *3. Virtual Vertigo*   *$30*   *$72*

Six passes to the new 3-D cinema ride in Times Square ($60) and a large pizza from Perfecto Pizza ($12). We recommend delaying pizza consumption until *after* the ride. This could be a fun birthday party.

☐ *4. Grub 'n Giggles*   *$40*   *$150*

Dinner for two at Isabella's ($100) and two tickets to Caroline's Comedy Club ($50), including two drinks each.

❁*❀*❁*❀*❁*❀*❁*❀*❁*❀*❁*❀*❁*❀*❁*❀*❁*❀*❁*❀*❁*❀*❁*❀*❁*❀*❁*❀*❁

Live Auction

❋*❀*❋*❀*❋*❀*❋*❀*❋*❀*❋*❀*❋*❀*❋*❀*❋*❀*❋*❀*❋*❀*❋*❀*

The Live Auction will begin at approximately 9:00 P.M., and what a show it will be! Harmer Johnson, a professional auctioneer, will describe the packages and will conduct the bidding process. There will be a minimum bid, usually 25 to 50% below the value, as shown in the catalogue. Bidders must raise their assigned Bidder ID above their heads, so the auctioneer can recognize your bid. The highest bid will be announced by the auctioneer and the winning Bidder ID will be recorded. You will pay for your items at the end of the evening. Cash, checks, and American Express will be accepted.

TIP:

• Remember to plan ahead with friends and family so that you can bid as a group, if you choose. This is an economical, fun, and practically way to bid. For example, if you want the Dessert of the Month, you can take six months and your friend can take six months. You each then pay half.

☐*1. For Bed or Wall, Most Magnificent of All...*   *Priceless*

are the four quilts made by Ms. Eisenberg, Ms. Tepper, Ms. Tyler, and Mr. Aherne's classes. Each quilt is different, made of squares done by the students and assembled by a quilting committee of parents. They will be auctioned individually throughout the evening.

☐*2. Tourist for a day*   *Estimated Value* **$190**

You're from Kankakee, visiting for the weekend. What do you do? Dinner for two at the Hard Rock Cafe ($50) and a couple of tickets to Beauty and the Beast ($140).

☐*3. Very Camp*   **$700**

Send a kid to day camp for three weeks this summer at A.C.T., the summer camp at the Cathedral of Saint John the Divine. This is for performing arts and sports.

☐*4. Catskill High*   **$250**

Flee the big city for a weekend at the 1830's farmhouse of Sam and Joyce Liberto. There are four bedrooms on a working farm just 20 minutes from the Baseball Hall of Fame, 10 minutes to Scotch Valley ski area, and closer still to lots of other good stuff. Any season. Call to schedule a mutually convenient weekend. The house-keys and directions are waiting.

☐*5. Sunday Brunch*   **$215**

Lisa Nord makes brunch for eight, home baked with Bloody Marys, waffles, fruit and more. Plus a prepared fruit basket from Mani's Market. This went for $375 at our last auction — a steal!

❋*❀*❋*❀*❋*❀*❋*❀*❋*❀*❋*❀*❋*❀*❋*❀*❋*❀*❋*❀*❋*❀*❋*❀*

7

■ ■ ■

Computers at School

1. Does the school have a computer lab with money for software?
2. Is there a computer teacher in the lab?
3. Does your school have at least one computer in every classroom? Does each computer have a CD-ROM player?
4. Does every classroom teacher know how to use the computer?
5. Do the teachers who use the computers use them to enhance the curriculum, or only for playing computer games?
6. Does the school have Internet/Intranet access?
7. If so, do the students use educational browsers?
8. Do students create homepages and send and receive E-mail?
9. Are word processing and touch typing being taught?
10. Does the school teach Logo, MicroWorlds, or similar programs designed to encourage logical thinking?

11. Is there a technology committee of parents and teachers?
12. Are there scanners to put children's drawings and writings into the school's site or individual classroom site?
13. Do the older students use the Internet or CD-ROM encyclopedias for research projects?
14. Does your school district have access to distance learning?
15. Are female students encouraged to learn computers in the same way that male students are?
16. Can the classroom teachers use their computers to access gradewide curricula and send E-mail to each other, improving teaching methods by easily sharing information?

Questions like these are useful for elementary school principals, technology committees, and school management councils who want to evaluate what and how students are being taught about technology in school. They can also be used by parents who want to make sure their children are acquiring computer skills in school. Today's schools cannot ignore technology; computer technology is becoming more sophisticated and more a part of our lives every day. It must be part of a basic education for today's children.

Children need to be taught competence in the functions of computers. Unlike their parents' generation, many of whom have been slower to adjust to computers, young children can learn technology quickly and need to be taught to use a computer as easily as they use a pencil and a piece of paper.

WHY CHILDREN SHOULD LEARN TO USE COMPUTERS IN SCHOOL

Computers can increase children's self-confidence by providing information sources at their fingertips. Drills in math, spelling, reading, and other basics are more fun using computers, making it more likely that children will do the work. Children are naturally curious, and computers can quickly satisfy their curiosity about a world of subjects. Vast amounts of information and knowledge that they may not get from textbooks and other traditional learning tools are available on the Internet, in library databases, and through links to other information resources.

Computers can make learning in all areas easier, especially in problem solving and language development. Computers can be used in creative ways that older children themselves initiate if they are given open-ended assignments. These go beyond basic drills and regular curriculum content. Children in poorer areas of the country need to grow up with a mouse in their hand as much, if not more, than more affluent children. These children are not as likely to be exposed to PCs at home. They need the hands-on instruction that can be taught in school or they will be at a serious disadvantage in later schooling, and when they enter the world of work. Being computer literate is necessary for more interesting higher-paying jobs.

Although many schools have acquired computers and networking capability, sophisticated equipment alone is not enough. Schools need computer-literate teachers who know how to use computers in their classrooms. If the teachers in your school are not computer-literate, how can the children hope to learn to use computers?

Parents can help schools move toward using technology. Parents with computer skills can help upgrade the technology in their schools; they can offer to tutor teachers if necessary. They can also write grants for technology projects. They can wire networks, repair computers, install software, create home pages, and set up media centers. Technology is always changing, and parents who have up-to-date skills in software, networking and other areas can contribute what they have learned at work or at home to their children's education.

If your school does not have computer-savvy parents, seek expert help from your school district, community-based organizations, corporations, or foundations. Use the quiz at the beginning of this chapter as a guide to get as much as you can for your school. In the winter, volunteers wire schools during an annual Net Day. Information on dates and supplies is available at 1-888-786-3897, or on the Web at http://www.netday.org.

HOW TO GET COMPUTERS FOR YOUR SCHOOL

If your school hasn't enough computers and is located near one or more large corporations, contact them and ask for donations of their older computers when they upgrade. Corporations frequently give away computers that are practically new. Used equipment can be a low-cost way to get started with computers, or an effective way to add a backup computer to a classroom.

Corporations, parents, or neighbors will want to donate used computers to the school to get a tax write-off, but schools should be cautious. While it is possible to take good parts from broken equipment and use them in working computers, don't accept computers that do not work unless you have parents or staff who have the time and skill to fix them. It can be very tempting to take anything that is offered, but the school can accumulate a large stockpile of useless, broken computers very quickly.

Older computers—usually more than three years—often don't work well because the new software the children will be using will not run on many older machines. It can be frustrating for teachers and students to have computers that are very slow, do not run the software, or break down easily. Having similar platforms, such as all Macintoshes, all IBM PCs or all PC clones can make it easier for the teachers and students to share software knowledge on a gradewide basis.

Partnerships That Can Provide Computers

The professional business associations in your area such as Lions, Kiwanis, Rotary, Small Business Association, or the Chamber of Commerce might be willing to donate money or computer equipment to your school. Another source of computers is your state education department that can be contacted through your school district. As well, large computer manufacturers, such as IBM, or software manufacturers, such as Microsoft Corp., might be willing to donate equipment or software to your school.

Money is available from Apple Computer Inc. for schools that form a technology partnership with a local college or university. These grants are on a large scale and require research into curricula that would be of interest to both the school and the college partner. These technology partnership grants are usually awarded for a two-year project and are highly competitive.

Contacting both Apple and IBM to get information on possible funding can be a way to get more computers, scanners, servers, software, and training for the school. The phone number for Apple Computer in Cupertino, California, is 1-408-996-1010. The phone number for IBM is 1-800-772-2227.

These are the two main computer makers, but there are many other smaller companies such as Dell, Compaq, and Packard Bell, that might give advice and information to schools. Contacting the computer resellers and national software retailers can sometimes provide good results. Some of the many companies include The Wiz, Egghead, CompUSA, Software Etc, and Computerland.

Getting Free Software and Training for Your School

Microsoft offers free Family Technology Nights in schools across the country. During these two-hour evenings, a computer specialist brings computers into the school and demonstrates safe use of the Internet and some of the latest features of on-line encyclopedias. Teachers are welcome and the school gets free software for hosting the event. Children get hands-on time to test the latest educational software. Advice on buying a computer is also offered to families.

These evenings are very popular and are designed to be strictly educational, not promotional. A Family Technology Night can be arranged with Microsoft by calling them at 1-800-203-5520, or via their website at www.microsoft.com.

COMPUTER LABS

It is possible to lease a large number of computers to equip a computer lab. The PTA at PS 75 leases thirty-two Macintosh computers on a yearly basis for their school's lab. Macintosh computers are found in most schools because they are easy for young children to use and are easy to maintain.

Leasing computers for a computer lab makes sense for a number of reasons. One big advantage is that the school can exchange all the computers after four years for new computers. Thus, after four years, the school is not stuck with a lab that won't run new software. Old computers are worth next to nothing in resale. Leasing also makes it possible to put twenty to thirty-five new computers in a lab by spending $8,000 to $12,000 a year instead of $20,000 to $35,000 all at once. Be sure to insure the computers in the lab with a separate insurance policy. Apple Computer and other manufacturers such as IBM or Compac can recommend third-party leasing companies to contact for more information.

In a lab it is advantageous for all the computers to be the same, not only for teaching large groups of children simultaneously, but also for maintenance reasons. A large TV screen in the lab helps with demonstrations for the entire class. A lending library is important, so classroom teachers can check out software for use in individual classes.

Computer Labs Teach Basic Computer Competence

This overview of minimum basic skills taught in computer labs was written by Sam Liberto, computer teacher at PS 75.

Kindergartners should be able to:

Enjoy computers, be familiar with the keyboard and mouse, and understand how to use three simple programs that support learning skills.

First-Graders should be able to:

Use CD-ROM books interactively, type simple stories into the computer, and use five or more simple programs that support curriculum areas.

Second-Graders should be able to:

Type a very short story into the computer, manipulate ten or more programs that support curriculum areas, and use programs to support math, reading, and science skills.

Third-Graders should be able to:

Type a one-page story into the computer, manipulate fifteen programs that support curriculum areas, begin to use multimedia presentation programs, and electronically communicate with teachers and other students in school.

Fourth-Graders should be able to:

Type, edit, and format a one-page story on the computer, manipulate twenty programs including reference programs, use a multimedia presentation program with assistance, and electronically communicate globally using project-net programs.

Fifth-Graders should be able to:

Type, edit, format a one- to two-page story and add graphics, use multimedia presentation programs unassisted to display learning, electronically communicate (using the World Wide Web) for reference, and use the computer to solve math, science, and logic problems.

Types of Computer Training for Teachers

Sometimes teachers are hesitant to use computers in the classroom. This can happen for many valid reasons, including lack of time to take classes, little knowledge of resources that could include the computer in the curriculum, or inability to fix a problem when the computer breaks down. There are many ways to overcome this hesitation. One solution is to hire a computer specialist who is willing to work with each teacher on a one-to-one basis, teaching them whatever they need to know. Individual training can help teachers answer specific questions in a hands-on, relaxed atmosphere. This has many advantages, including eliminating possible embarrassment of the teacher. If necessary the PTA can pay for this training, or the principal may have a training budget that can be used for this purpose.

Another solution is teachers mentoring each other. Teachers can share their knowledge of new software on a grade-wide basis or on an individual basis.

TECHNOLOGY COMMITTEES

Some schools have a technology committee made up of teachers, parents, and principal or assistant principal. This committee meets regularly to decide all issues related to computers in the school. Parents concerned about what is available on the Internet seek an active role in setting policies for student use. Guidelines regarding home pages, restrictions on the use of student photos, and other issues affecting student safety are set by parents and teachers together. Computer curriculum recommendations and expectations for competence on each grade level can also be agreed upon in the technology committee.

A parents' computer repair and support group, which supplies parent technical help for each classroom teacher, can be organized through the technology committee. Parents who can fix technical problems can provide invaluable help. Establish such a committee by checking through parent surveys handed out early in the year, or by sending home a note to parents in the class, asking for help. A knowledgeable parent volunteer can also teach new software or use of the computer to the classroom teacher and to the children.

COMPUTERS IN THE CLASSROOM

The computer as a tool for learning in the classroom is most effective when it is well integrated into the curriculum. A cooperative relationship between the classroom teachers and the computer lab teacher is essential to this integration. The lab teacher is a resource for all the classroom teachers, since software catalogs and other computer-related information are received by the lab teacher on a regular basis.

At the end of this chapter there is a chart of suggested software programs for each grade level put together by Dr. Mary Rojas, a parent member of the PS 75 technology committee. The format of the chart helps pinpoint what educational goal each software program supports. Many of these programs are still available, but other, more recent software programs could be substituted using these catagories as a guide.

An Expert's Opinion on What Children Can Learn From Computers

In 1980 Seymour Papert, now the Lego Chair at MIT, wrote a book called *Mindstorms: Children, Computers and Powerful Ideas.* One of the ideas in his book is that children learn by doing. To this end, Mr. Papert created Logo, a child-friendly programming language designed to help kids think logically. This fifteen-year-old language and the more recent language, MicroWorlds, are open-ended tools. Schools that teach these languages find them powerful learning tools for older elementary children. More information can be obtained by calling The Logo Foundation (212-579-8028).

Mr. Papert has also written a new book called *The Connected Family,* published by Longstreet Press, which gives parents advice on raising computer-literate children. Here are his personal criteria for selecting sound software:

1. Is the toy running the child, or is the child running the toy? Papert does not like software that treats children as if they were answering machines, learning facts without skills. The best learning comes at some effort, not disguised as a game.
2. Is there room for fantasy making, make-believe, and imagination as well as facts and skill? Logo and Microworlds are good examples of how you can learn facts while you're in a make-believe environment.
3. Is there something to share? Good examples are software programs that let you make a picture, a card, or a project.
4. Try it before you buy it. If after five minutes you can't understand anything about what's going on—that's bad. But if after five minutes you understand everything, that's worse.

Papert's book is about parenting in high-tech times. For a review, read the February 1997 issue of *Family PC Magazine,* in which editor Robin Raskin interviewed Mr. Papert, in "Computing's Idealist." Visit the Family PC website at www.familypc.com.

THE INTERNET

The Internet is a hot topic in schools these days. President Clinton and Vice President Gore are encouraging parents and other volunteers to wire local schools for access to this information source. Many governors have organized Net Days, opening school buildings and providing supplies in an effort to speed up the process of providing Internet access. Many schools have been wired or are scheduled to be wired in 1997–98. The FCC will make 2.25 billion dollars available to schools annually for Internet-access wiring. Information about future Net Days is available at 1-888-786-3897.

Use of the Internet in schools is an equity issue that politicians are supporting, and rightly so. Schools in poor districts or isolated areas can and need to have access to the same E-mail capabilities, databases and website links as schools in more affluent areas.

Using the Internet Safely at Home

The following tips on safe use of the Internet for families and kids were taken from "The Parent's Guide to the Information Superhighway: Rules and Tools for Families Online," a thirty-six-page booklet available from The Children's Partnership at 310-260-1220 or on-line at www.childrenspartnership.org. The Children's Partnership educates policy makers and parents about technology issues affecting children; the Partnership works to ensure that technology and quality content are available to all children. It also publishes briefing materials and operates a website for parents.

A Parent's Checklist

Tap your child's natural sense of wonder and discovery and temper it with your experience and counsel.

Let your child take the lead, but stay with him or her until you've decided the activity is appropriate.

Spend as much "cyber-time" with your child as you can and bookmark your favorite sites.

Provide your child with clear, simple instructions about how to avoid danger and what to do if something happens: Who to speak to, etc.

Set limits appropriate to your child's age.

Talk to your child often about his or her computer or on-line life.

Monitor, monitor, monitor (time, phone bills, chat groups, and on-screen materials).

Use on-line experiences as another way to teach responsibility, good conduct, and values.

Share an E-mail address with your child, so you can oversee his or her mail and discuss correspondence.

Instruct your child not to order products or give out information about themselves or their family without your permission.

Teach your child to let you know if they encounter anything scary or unusual on-line.

Be sure your child understands the actions that can be taken if people harass them on-line or do anything inappropriate.

Parents may want to post the following list near the computer.

A Young Person's Guide to Safe Use of the Internet

Always tell your parents or another adult immediately if something is confusing or seems scary or threatening.

Don't give out your full name, real address, telephone number, school name or location, schedule, password, or other identifying information when you're on-line. Check with an adult for any exceptions.

Never have a face-to-face meeting with someone you've met on-line. In rare cases, your parents may decide it's okay, but if you do decide to meet a cyberpal, make sure you meet in a public place and that a parent or other adult is with you.

Never respond on-line to any messages that use bad words or words that are scary, threatening, or just feel weird. If you get that kind of a message, print it out or make a copy, and tell an adult immediately.

Never go into a new on-line area that is going to cost additional money without first asking permission from your parent or teacher.

Never send a picture over the Internet or via regular mail to anyone without your parent's permission.

Don't give out a credit card number on-line.

DESIGNING A SCHOOL HOMEPAGE OR WEBSITE

Each school can have its own website, or home page, designed by parents, teachers, or students. The following is a list of links to a school's website that could be useful to students and parents. These ideas came from Howard Leib, a parent at PS 75 who is interested in creating websites. Keeping the site up-to-date is necessary for it to be useful. This updating can be done by several people, each responsible for a separate area, or by one person willing to call all committee heads for updates. The PS 75 website can be found at www.webcom.com/PS75.

Home Page: This is the opening page for the school, providing links to other sites.

Principal's Office: Greetings from the Principal, announcements.

Classrooms: Each class is responsible for its own page, with student work, class parent information, announcements.

After-School Program: Schedules, rules, registration forms, contacts for the program.

PTA: Minutes from meetings, announcements, committee contacts.

Bulletin Board: Monthly calendars, notices, special events.

School Phone Directory: Directory of classroom extensions, school numbers (not a directory of student phone numbers).

Cafeteria: The school lunch menu, information about federal free lunch program, rules of behavior in the lunchroom.

School Planning Council: Minutes, schedules, school mission statement, next meeting's agenda.

Teacher's Room: Links to curriculum sites.

Parent's Room: Links to parenting sites.

Playground: Favorite sites for kids.

School District Office: Contact information, schedules.

Homework Help: Link to homework-related resources.

Library: Information on library use, book reviews by students in the school, and links to related sites (Scholastic, HarperKids).

BEYOND THE COMPUTER: DISTANCE LEARNING

Distance learning is a new use of technology that is available in many parts of the country through service providers. The system makes available specialists who are highly skilled in their curriculum areas. Scientists, mathematicians, and others well-known in their fields tailor lessons to teachers and students, thereby raising the level of education offered in schools.

District 3 in New York City has recently become part of a project to install satellite dishes on top of five participating schools in the district. Each classroom teacher in the school is supplied with access to a computer, a TV monitor, a VCR, a telephone and a fax machine.

When a teacher is teaching part of a curriculum subject and wants to include more information, she can fax a request to project headquarters. This request usually describes the curriculum area the children are working on and asks for resources such as lesson plans, training tapes, and a list of books or tapes for reference. The teacher might also ask to have a master in the field teach the class—or the teacher—with a live broadcast. This technology can quickly communicate the latest advanced teaching techniques, expanding the quality of the information children receive.

The next level of sophistication in this technology is interactive distance learning. This kind of program is especially good for schools like Kula School in Maui, where the children are physically isolated from the rest of the country. It can also make a huge difference in the quality of education in poor neighborhoods of large cities or remote rural areas. Schools can choose to communicate with cultural institutions, hospitals, museums, or other participating members. Each of these participating members must have the same equipment and hookups in order to broadcast and receive transmissions from schools.

To set up interactive distance learning, a school needs a special room for transmitting from the school. Proper acoustic soundproofing, video cameras, microphones, and approximately nine large TV monitors are needed. Also needed is a multi-channel video cable called a DS3 with an embedded T-1 line for quick communication. It is an expensive program that needs to be paid for by large corporate or government grants.

This setup might be used so that a local public school could receive instruction from a master teacher at a professional ballet company in New York City. The teacher would demonstrate a routine in front of the camera in her Lincoln Center studio; students would then try out the routine in front of their school's camera. The transmission time is so fast that there is little delay for either the children or the teacher. It is as if the teacher and the students are in the same room. The possibilities are unlimited for this type of technology in the schools.

COMPUTER USE AT TWO SCHOOLS

Technology at Beverly Farms Elementary

At Beverly Farms, parents have played a large role in the development of the technology area of the school. When the governor of Maryland declared a Net Weekend in 1997, parents and local volunteers saved the school thousands of dollars by wiring the building themselves for access to the Internet.

The Media Center is the new name for a school library in Montgomery County schools. At Beverly Farms, there is a cluster of computers on one wall where students can use either Netscape Navigator or Scholastic Browser to comb the Internet for age-appropriate educational information. Books in the Media Center are checked out using a laser scanner, which reads the bar code taped to each book. When a student checks out a book, the due date and the student's name are stored in the system. Students can then find out whether a book is checked out from the Media Center by using their classroom computer to access the Media Center's book collection.

Every classroom has one or more computers and a printer. Some of the signs hanging in the hallway of the school pose computer-related questions to make students think about computer-related terms.

The PTA and principal cosponsor a monthly technology night at the school. During this evening, teachers and staff demonstrate the educational software currently being used in the classroom to interested parents and students. In addition to sponsoring regular technology nights, the PTA is currently running a pledge drive to buy twenty new computers for the lab.

The school has acquired computers when parents and relatives save cash-register receipts from the Giant Supermarket. The market is one of two in the area that offer hardware and software in exchange for receipts. Parents trade receipts from Safeway, the other supermarket, with parents from other schools who save those receipts. Parents persuade their co-workers to bring receipts to work. Check in your area to see if any of the markets have this kind of program for schools.

Parents Support Technology at Kula Elementary

Kula Elementary in Hawaii uses a local area network within the school and a wide-area network to connect the school's computers with the rest of the world. Each class has a minimum of two computers, one Macintosh hooked to the Internet and one for classroom projects. The school is now upgrading the machines in the computer lab, from its eight Macs and fourteen older Apple computers to new equipment.

In the Kula computer lab and in some of the classrooms, parents help the teacher with the computers, repairing hardware and debugging software problems. Parents are also helpful in acquiring more computers and software for the classrooms. Some of the computers in the school were purchased with state money, some from programs like the Foodland Shop for Better Education. Still others were obtained through grants and donations by businesses and organizations on the island.

A Final Word

Teachers need flexibility and help to keep pace with constantly changing new technologies. Administrators need to view computers as part of the basic curriculum of their school, just like reading and math.

Learning to use a computer and the related communication tools is a complicated process for both students and teachers. It can take a long time even with on-going training and it requires commitment to using the computer in everyday activities. This means a high level of cooperation between the lab teacher and classroom teachers so they can share the necessary information.

Some schools offer computer classes as if they were enrichment classes; but computer classes should be required for every student so that computer literacy is integrated into the schedule. This needs to be done without sacrificing the funding for art or music. Computer lab teachers are needed not only to teach basic literacy, but as resource people for computer use in the classrooms as well.

8

■ ■ ■

School Management Councils

A school management council is similar to a board of directors with parents, teachers and principals as board members. It is different from the PTA or other parent organization. Its responsibility is to set policies for the school that improve student achievement. Each individual school council decides how their school will implement policies that will improve student achievement. In this chapter we will look at examples of school councils from Kentucky and New York City.

KENTUCKY LEADS THE NATION

Since laws were passed creating school councils in states around the nation, the state of Kentucky has been at the forefront of the movement, creating very specific laws that govern their school councils. The law requires a yearly plan for all councils. After a plan is put together by the council in the summer, it is sent to civic and business leaders in the community. An open forum is held every fall at the school for public comments on the yearly plan.

Parent members of Kentucky councils are required by state law to receive the same training as the teachers. This training contains twelve modules, lasts six hours, and must be administered by a state-certified trainer. As a result, parent council members are as well-versed in the education laws as the teachers are.

Dry Ridge Elementary School

The Dry Ridge Elementary School Council started in 1990. The council is a model organization, which schools in other states are emulating. Constance Deats, the principal, has a number of years' experience as a state-certified trainer for school councils. Ms. Deats believes the principal's job is to run the school on a day-to-day basis, leaving the council free to focus on how to increase learning opportunities for the students. It is also the role of the principal to "keep folks moving forward," so the council doesn't get stuck on issues such as building cleanliness, discipline, or personal issues.

The Dry Ridge Council keeps the focus on improving student learning through curriculum and community involvement. (See also Introduction and Dry Ridge Elementary Executive Summary at the end of this chapter.) One exciting council project, part of a five-year plan, is called the Outdoor Classroom. This project is a joint effort of the council and the community. Plants and animals will be studied in this outdoor classroom by the students of Dry Ridge Elementary. This area will also be open to all members of the community for use as a recreational park. Everyone will benefit from this effort. Children from the school wrote a successful grant proposal for $1,000, which the council submitted to General Electric Corporation. The money helped underwrite the cost of creating three miles of hiking trails on the grounds of the school. Community volunteers donated lumber and built a gazebo.

The council also is currently working on a project to get migrant workers to enroll their children in school. Many workers do not speak English well and do not understand that their children can come to public school. Others are afraid because they do not have green cards. Ms. Deats goes to visit these migrant families accompanied by two Spanish-speaking PTA members. They encourage parents to register their children at Dry Ridge Elementary. They also explain that Dry Ridge has two computers devoted entirely to teaching English to Spanish-speaking adults and invite them to come to the school.

The council also approved the production of a video as a showcase for the school. The children and teachers wrote, acted, and produced the video that is given to new parents as an introduction to the school. It is also useful in introducing the school to community organizations and corporations who might be able to help the school with donations or volunteers.

SCHOOL MANAGEMENT COUNCILS IN NEW YORK

In March, 1991, the New York State Board of Regents adopted a document called, "A New Compact for Learning, Improving Public Elementary, Middle, and Secondary Education Results in the 1990s." Besides adopting new curriculum standards, this document made it possible for schools in New York State to develop school management councils. The Compact states that schools need "top-down support for bottom-up reform." Parents have long complained that legislators making decisions at the state level could not possibly understand the needs of their individual schools. The Compact allows all members of the school community to be heard and to make decisions that all agree are best for the students.

Parent Teacher Associations or other types of parents associations have no official decision-making authority in schools. Parent groups can organize, volunteer, fund-raise, and then decide with the principal how the money will be spent. But this collaboration is based on the good will between the principal and parents, not on the authority of the parent group to make decisions on how to run the school.

School management councils will not eliminate parents associations because both are needed in different capacities, despite the overlap of parent involvement. Parents will always need to have their own organization for supporting the schools. By law, council members are the principal, and equal numbers of teachers and parents. These councils give the teachers more of a voice and open a regular dialogue among principals, parents, and teachers, which a PTA does not provide.

Working on a school-based management council requires a large investment of time if the council is to be successful, often making it difficult to find council members. Constraints imposed by contracts with the teacher's union can limit what the council can do. In addition there are school district education policies that all schools must adhere to. In spite of these restrictions, school-based councils are the wave of the future. These groups will give new life to public schools in New York State, giving decision-making power to parents and teachers.

In New York State school councils will have the responsibility of allocating federal and state funds in the school starting in October 1999. They are responsible for creating a plan every year for the school. They draw up the budget and implement it.

How to Create a New School Council

Dr. Mary Rojas is a PS 75 parent and the chairperson of the School Management Council for the first three years of the group's existence. She stresses that creating a working council, which makes decisions in the best interest for the children in the school, can take two to four years. She outlined that process as she remembered it at the end of the third year of operation.

In the first year of the council, the members were optimistic that having this new group was an opportunity to set a new direction for the school. The hardest part at the beginning was building trust. The only ground rules for meetings were that they be very democratic, giving every person the right to speak. At the outset, the parent body was very outspoken and many teachers felt threatened by them. A few parents talked at length at every meeting. Teachers almost never spoke in the first year. They were skeptical about this new council and wondered if it was really going to accomplish anything, besides giving the parents another forum to criticize the school.

When teachers did not speak up in the group, the chairperson spoke individually to them outside of meetings, seeking their input. She was very careful never to express her opinion, so as not to sway the others.

With careful listening trust developed as time went by. During the second year, teachers started speaking out more openly. In fact, almost everyone wanted to share their ideas now. It became like a large group of noisy siblings, with each person trying to express his opinion, sometimes interrupting one another.

The chairperson came up with simple rules, which were approved by the council, for maintaining order.

No talking out of turn.
  Wait to be called on in order of request.
Respect the speaker.
No interruptions while someone else is speaking.
No third-person accounts of incidents in school. The purpose of this rule was to get rid of rumors.
No long speeches.

Each person is called on in the order on the list of people who want to speak, kept by one person. The list system keeps the more vocal people from monopolizing the meeting. The rules give the chairperson the authority to tell anyone unable to resolve a conflict in the meeting that they must leave.

During the third year, the group used more structured agendas and minutes. They created more formalized subcommittes to follow up on issues and report back to the council. The council was becoming a working forum for real change in the school. A formal vision statement was created and approved by the council. Issues such as class placement, equity, and report cards were discussed and recommendations from the council were implemented by the principal.

MEETING FORMAT

The group meets once a month on a Monday afternoon following the teachers' staff meeting. This schedule permits teachers to combine two meetings into one afternoon. The meetings last two hours and are open to any parent or teacher who would like to attend. The first half-hour is the business meeting where follow-up on committees occurs and new items are added to the agenda— three months in advance so they can be prioritized and scheduled for discussion.

For the next one-and-one-half hours the big agenda topics are discussed by both voting members, nonvoting members, and any visitors who want to speak up. The council does not formally vote but comes to consensus by a nod of heads. Coming to consensus involves the chairperson saying something like, "If you can't live with this, speak now." This formalizes the decision-making process, guaranteeing support from the members of the school council. To end the meeting the chairperson summarizes what has been discussed, suggests follow-up, and announces the agenda for the next meeting.

IMPORTANT ROLES WITHIN THE COUNCIL

A chairperson is the facilitator for the group. The role of the chairperson is to keep order, move things along, and bring discussions to consensus if possible. While this is an important role, no council should depend too heavily on one person, whether it is a parent or teacher chairperson. Because of this, the PS 75 council currently has co-chairs—a teacher and a parent. Changes in leadership styles from meeting to meeting can keep the council fresh, effective, and more representative of all points of view.

The Scribe takes notes in the meeting and has the responsibility of getting the minutes to the chairperson for revision and corrections. Minutes disseminators are responsible for translating the minutes into Spanish, putting them in simple grid form, copying them, sending them home to parents, and storing them in binders. The columns have headings such as Topic, Discussed, Voted On, and Follow-Up. They are also reponsible for posting them in the lobby for public viewing.

The Timekeeper allows three to five minutes per speaker. The Checker calls on people to speak in order and keeps them on the topic. The Reflector speaks at the end of the meeting to comment on the effectiveness of the meeting.

Sometimes subcommittes are needed to research, survey the school, or complete other tasks related to the work of the council. These subcommittees usually meet as needed, in addition to council sessions. Each subcommittee has both parent and teacher members.

HOW MEMBERS ARE CHOSEN TO BE ON THE COUNCIL

The council holds elections for new members in October. In September parents who have the time and interest to participate are encouraged to run. Short statements from each candidate in English and Spanish are posted in the lobby and sent home for parents to read. Because PS 75 has a student population of more than 700 students in K–5, six parents and two alternates and six teachers and two alternates represent the different groups in the school. Staggered two-year terms are being considered in the future for continuity and fresh perspectives from new parents and teachers.

It is impossible to predict who will be elected, but it is good for parents to keep in mind when voting that the council should be representative of the entire school. Special education, dual language, different ethnic backgrounds, and other groups need be represented. Ballots are sent home in Spanish and English and are due back in one week.

When the votes are sent back in, they are counted by teachers and parents together. The six with the most votes are elected as regular parent members. Alternates are the two with the next highest number of votes. The teachers elect their own members and alternates. The entire process can take two weeks.

ISSUES ADDRESSED IN COUNCIL MEETINGS

First year of operation:

West Side Academy restructuring and creating a vision

K–5 restructuring, creating a vision, submitted a grant proposal to organize the school into smaller units of K–2 and 3–5

Coordination of teacher and classroom supplies with school ordering and scavenger hunt

Computer Fix-It Day. Parents and computer technicians got together to diagnose and repair all the computers in school.

School Discipline

Safety in the school yards during lunch

How to ease the lunch madness

The entire school's library needs

Second year of operation:

Classroom placement

Report card format (K–2 and 3–5)

School budget

Technology

Equity

Restructuring

Principal selection

Third Year of operation:

Vision Statement

Curriculum standards

Report Cards
Constitution
Evaluation of programs in school
Classroom placement (after new principal arrived)
Equity (after new principal)

PUBLIC SCHOOL 75 VISION STATEMENT CREATED BY THE COUNCIL

PS 75, the Emily Dickinson School, is a neighborhood school in District 3 that truly reflects the rich diversity of our community.

Our children are taught to be confident and skilled in reading, writing, mathematics, social studies, science, and technology. Students are offered a rich, interdisciplinary experience in the arts, taking advantage of the wealth of cultural opportunities available in our city.

PS 75 provides a safe and nurturing environment, where children with a wide range of abilities and talents can flourish. At PS 75, education is a partnership built on strong collaboration among faculty members, parents, and children. Family involvement and support is essential.

Our children learn to be cooperative and respectful, to resolve conflicts creatively, and to build community while appreciating differences. They are taught to think critically, analyze carefully, and communicate clearly. Our school inspires a lifelong love of learning.

School management councils are the wave of the future for the public schools. They are a very useful tool for fostering communication and cooperation among those involved. Effective councils address and solve problems related to student achievement and well being. As more schools around the country establish councils, public education will undoubtedly improve.

INTRODUCTION

WELCOME TO THE TRANSFORMATION PLAN FOR DRY RIDGE ELEMENTARY SCHOOL. IT IS OUR VISION, AS REPRESENTATIVES FOR THE PARENTS AND EDUCATORS OF OUR SCHOOL, THAT THIS PLAN PROVIDES A CHALLENGE FOR EACH INDIVIDUAL TO REACH THEIR MAXIMUM POTENTIAL THROUGH DEVELOPMENTALLY APPROPRIATE PROGRAMS DESIGNED TO MEET THE NEEDS OF THE WHOLE CHILD. WE TRUST THAT YOU WILL FIND IT TO BE AMBITIOUS FOR STUDENTS AND CHALLENGING FOR THE FACULTY, STAFF, ADMINISTRATION, PARENTS AND COMMUNITY. WE HOPE YOU WILL FIND ACTIVITIES THAT YOU CAN JOIN AND SUPPORT.

THIS PLAN IS A COMMITMENT TO TRANSFORM DRY RIDGE ELEMENTARY SCHOOL. WITHOUT FUNDAMENTAL CHANGE IN THE WAY WE TEACH, LEARN. AND PARENT, DRY RIDGE STUDENTS WILL NOT MEET THE HIGH STANDARDS CALLED FOR BY THE GENERAL ASSEMBLY IN THE KENTUCKY EDUCATION REFORM ACT.

THE SCHOOL WILL CHANGE, ONLY IF EACH OF US CHANGE. WE SALUTE YOUR WILLINGNESS TO BECOME A LEARNER AS WELL AS PARENT, ADMINISTRATOR, TEACHER OR STUDENT.

BEST WISHES,

THE DRY RIDGE ELEMENTARY SCHOOL COUNCIL

NANCY G. DULEY, PRINCIPAL

JUDY CONRAD, TEACHER

BARBARA PACE, PARENT

MARCELLA SOPER, TEACHER

ED LORENZ, PARENT

EDNA WHALEY, TEACHER

DRY RIDGE ELEMENTARY
EXECUTIVE SUMMARY

The purpose of the Dry Ridge Elementary Transformation Plan is to evaluate and improve the programs, communication, and strategies used to promote opportunities to all students for advancement toward their potential through developmentally appropriate practices. It is our desire to instill the skills for life long learning.

The planning process included all stakeholders in the school through the use of: committees with parental and community involvement, surveys (student, parent and teacher), results of assessment data, and the assistance of the administration. All other school plans are embedded within the context of this plan. The evaluation and communication of the plan will be a priority and a continuous process each year.

The following areas were identified for improvement:

Writing:
- Staff training in analyzing open-response/ended questions in all content areas.
- Teachers will administer sample open-response/ended questions and analyze them in a group meeting.
- Every level will complete a student writing portfolio.
- Each family/grade level will review their teacher portfolios twice a year to identify instructional strengths and weakensses.

Math:
- Students will participate in activities requiring them to create and interpret diagrams, charts, graphs, etc.
- Students will participate in activities concentrating on appropriate Math and KIRIS terminology.
- Teachers will participate in math training aligned with KERA Goals and National Math Standards.
- Students will participate in Extended School Service targeting problem solving and critical thinking skills in math.
- Students will participate in activities using various types of calculators.
- Students will have practice in exploration, selection, and application of appropriate computational operations to solve real life problems.

- Students will practice writing math responses to multiple part questions.

Science:
- Teachers will participate in district-wide work sessions to align science curriculum with KERA Goals and National Standards.
- An updated resource pool of educators and community resource persons will be identified and invited to share the importance of science in their vocations.
- Teachers who have been to science workshops will share ideas with the staff at regularly scheduled bimonthly staff meetings.
- Students will present examples of science experiments at designated PTA meetings.

Character Education:
- A committee consisting of PTA representative, parents, counselor, faculty, staff, custodians, lunchroom workers, and bus drivers will be formed to create a school-wide character education program.
- All faculty, staff, custodians, lunchroom workers, and bus drivers will receive a verbal explanation and written summary of the school-wide character education program containing specific ideas and activities to be used by them.
- Students will participate in a school-wide character education program.
- Students will be taught through a curriculum integrated with each concept of character education.
- Students will be participating in at least 3 activities from each concept area of character education.

Art:
- An art consultant will develop a school-wide program focusing on strategies for teaching sequential elements of art.
- Students will participate in weekly hands-on activities using the sequential elements of art.

Evaluation of Student Learning:
- A form will be designed to show the change in scores for the total student population of each level or grade as they move from year to year.
- Results of the Test of Cognitive Skills (TCS), California Tests of Basic

Skils (CTBS) and Kentucky Instructional Results Information System (KIRIS) will be used to evaluate student retention and learning of material and will be shared at parent conferences.

- Students in each level and grade will take pre-tests in appropriate areas and results will be shared with parents.
- Students in each level and grade will take post-tests in appropriate areas and results will be shared with parents.

9
■ ■ ■

Safety Issues

Safety is always a concern for parents of elementary and middle school children. You don't have to look farther than your morning milk carton highlighting the faces of missing children. Parents want to keep their children safe, especially in their own neighborhood. Recent studies have shown that in neighborhoods that watch over the children, crime rates involving children are lower. This is good news. Although the cycle of poverty in inner-city neighborhoods and some rural areas is hard to break, neighbors can do something about crimes involving children: They can make the resources of the neighborhood accessible to them. Parents and concerned neighbors can develop a neighborhood safety program modeled on sucessful programs such as Safe Haven.

SAFE HAVEN SAFETY PROGRAM FOR CHILDREN

The Safe Haven Program on the Upper West Side of Manhattan is a thirteen-year-old, child-safety program. It started in 1984 as a Parents' Association program; since 1991 it has been based in two local nonprofit organizations, Westside Crime Prevention Program and The Resourceful Family.

Safe Haven is an excellent example of school involvement spreading into the community at large. Today's parents and children take its programs for granted, enjoying the family atmosphere of this urban neighborhood. But the Upper West Side had not always been so child friendly or so safe. The Safe Haven story is about a dynamic partnership between parents, teachers, and children. It's about a group of individuals who devoted years to making the program survive and thrive. Mostly it's about people inspiring each other to get involved and do something about a problem nagging at everyone's peace of mind.

It started when a teacher overheard two students talking about a man who seemed to have followed them as they walked to school. The teacher acted immediately, talking to the students, bringing in the police, and telling parents in the school's Parents Association of the incident. A meeting was held, at which another teacher noted that students in the school had also been upset about mistreatment in a local store; they had told parents, but no one had taken action.

The Parents' Association mobilized quickly, realizing the problem was not just the threat of crime, but that students didn't know what to do when a situation looked threatening. The Parents' Association president recruited a parent leader. Within a month, she started a school store, so students wouldn't feel compelled to shop at the local store that had been a problem. She brought in the police to train children and parents in basic crime-prevention skills; she also started a school patrol made up of parent volunteers. The patrol was necessary because the school doors had faulty locks and parents and teachers were nervous about intruders getting into the building. Her most far-reaching effort, however, was to reactivate a neighborhood child-safety program called the Safe Haven merchant program. To do this, she formed an alliance with an interested private-school representative who agreed to organize private school parents to contact merchants. At the time only one local store had a Safe Haven decal.

The basic idea of the Safe Haven program was that a child who felt threatened by a stranger, was injured, or who had some other reason for seeking shelter, could go into a neighborhood store that displayed a bright yellow SAFE HAVEN decal. These decals were placed at a child's eye level and could be seen from outside the store. The decal made it easy for children to identify a friendly store, providing safety for the youngster and giving free access to a telephone. This program is invaluable in urban neighborhoods, particularly when children go to and from school alone.

The public school parent and the private school representative each made phone calls to parents at neighborhood schools and local business organizations to expand the merchant program. As a result of the calls, a parent at another school called a press conference to which fifteen newspapers and radio stations responded. Another parent performed at local street fairs dressed as the Safe Haven clown. All the publicity helped get more schools to participate. The local Chamber of Commerce contributed $500 for Safe Haven decals, and the effort began to snowball. Parents from private, parochial, and public schools recruited merchants and posted decals on handpicked stores on streets they knew well. They also provided important training materials and got feedback. Getting twenty different schools involved made this truly a neighborhood program.

Meanwhile, back at PS 75, one of the teachers, who had been especially supportive of all this activity, encouraged the Parents' Association president to write a grant proposal to the New York State Division of Criminal Justice Service. Because the Safe Haven Merchants program was growing rapidly, money was needed to maintain and continue to expand it. Winning the award of $7,000 gave recognition and legitimacy that was crucial for working with government agencies.

Strengthened by the grant, the following year the school was able to hire consultants who specialized in training children and parents about crimes—perpetrated by strangers or by family members. The Parents' Association also decided the children should train each other by creating a video.

The Parents' Association president, who was now the director of the Child Safety Program, engaged the safety consultants to work with writing teachers from Teachers and Writers Collaborative and a selected group of students on a script for a safety video for children. The grant paid for a videocamera, and a video director from Teachers and Writers, while volunteers coordinated endless details. The final product was called "Streetwise and Safe," an entertaining and informative video, student-written and performed. This video features tips like how to use a pay phone even if the child has no money, how to avoid a stranger who seems to be following them, and how to deal with bullies on the street. It is still the backbone of child-training sessions held in Manhattan neighborhood schools.

The problem of the school doors still needed attention. But what do you do when an enormous public school system already has hundreds of complaints for physical repairs? Roll in the squeaky wheel with a lot of networking and pressure. Here was a school where parents had clearly indicated their involvement by spending hundreds of volunteer hours in a patrol and complex security analysis that was all a necessity because the eight exit doors didn't lock. Realizing that a lawsuit could be brought against it, the Board of Education soon replaced the sticky, old, warped wooden doors with sturdy metal ones, that clicked neatly and safely into place. Suddenly a sympathetic and delighted district superintendent was posting visitor security signs and security personnel at schools throughout the district.

Meanwhile the Parents' Association president kept writing grant proposals, and expanding the program throughout the neighborhood. The Upper West Side had 30,000 children—a big population to protect! New York State limits an organization to five years of funding, and the Child Safety Program, which won the state's award for best community crime-prevention program, kept up the proposals, got the grants for the considerably larger funds needed each year, and wrote and filed quarterly reports, vouchers, and other necessary paperwork. However, it became clear that one more program was needed to make this Child Safety Program as comprehensive as possible.

The Parents' Association decided to start a basketball league, called the Safe Haven West Side Basketball League. It was intended to keep children busy and active on weekends during the long winter months. It was an activity in which families of all different backgrounds and economic levels could get to know each other. Games would be played in public school gyms and would be coached by parent volunteers working with hundreds of children. New York Criminal Justice Services provided the seed money to cover these initial costs, the biggest of which was rental of public school gyms. The shirts, which the hundreds of children in the program would wear, would publicize the Safe Haven program, and let everyone know that this is a family neighborhood where people were pulling together to make children feel safe, and happy.

Running all of this was too much for one Parents' Association to handle. It was time to find a home for the Child Safety Program. West Side Crime Prevention took over the Safe Haven merchant program and training. A local nonprofit called The Resourceful Family, specializing in youth recreation, became the umbrella organization for the basketball league.

This entirely volunteer-run league, headed by director Eileen Palley, now has twelve divisions (four for girls and eight for boys) for a total of 700 children ages eight to seventeen, who come from public, private, and parochial schools. It continues to be supported by neighborhood merchants and corporate sponsors. Each season ends with a series of eight gala, potluck suppers in public school cafeterias. And everyone there marvels at the reality, that it's possible to create a family neighborhood, once we realize that the supposedly "at risk" children are ours.

Over 500 volunteers have been extraordinary in their generosity with time in order to make this process a success. Some of the key people were: Jane Mushabac, Brenda Epstein, Mayra Fernandez, Eugenia Triay, Violet Guerin, Marsha Hurst, and Eileen Palley. They are mothers, fathers, teachers, community leaders, merchants, the people who shared a vision for a whole neighborhood and devoted themselves to doing what it took to make that vision a reality: calling meetings, writing proposals and reports, leading the safety patrol, running the school store, producing the video, running a huge basketball league, visiting every Safe Haven merchant, translating materials into Spanish and Korean, lobbying for assistance, improving school building security, bringing in the press, and coordinating with Albany personnel, the Board of Education, local police, and new umbrella organizations.

WEST SIDE CRIME PREVENTION

West Side Crime Prevention Program (WCPP) is a neighborhood non-profit organization which works closely with the local police, schools, and the entire neighborhood to keep crime down. WCPP has been run since its inception by Margorie Cohen and Tamar Lynn, two extradordinary women. Besides administering the Safe Haven Stores Program, representatives from WCPP go to schools, speaking to parents and students about how children can travel safely in the neighborhood, avoiding crime. This program is called "Being Streetwise and Safe" and includes the video that was made by the PS 75 students several years ago. WCPP works with the police to create "safe corridors" near schools that are regularly patrolled by the police for children walking to and from school. WCPP works with public and private schools to help them organize parent safety patrols.

WCPP sends a policeman to neighborhood middle schools and high schools to work with the guidance counselors on student conflict resolution. This program is called Resolution Is the Solution and includes role-playing, a twelve-minute video on conflict resolution, and a question-and-answer period with a retired policeman. The twofold purpose of the program first teaches students to resolve conflicts themselves nonviolently, and second that the police are their friends, not their enemies.

Police departments in many areas of the country have similar community service programs that send the police directly to the schools. Check with your local police department about existing crime-prevention and safety programs in your area. For more information on making your neighborhood safer for everyone, contact Marjorie Cohen, Executive Director, West Side Crime Prevention, 891 Amsterdam Avenue, Room 106, New York, N.Y. 10025, 212-866-8603. She will be happy to discuss solutions and give advice on setting up a program similar to any of the successful ones that WCPP operates.

List of Resources for Parents on Child Safety Issues

The National Safe Kids Campaign at 202-884-4993 for childhood injury prevention information and materials.

National PTA, Health Programs 330 N. Wabash, Suite 2100, Chicago, Illinois 60611 for information on "Follow the Rules Bus Safety Program" and "The Way to Ride a Bicycle Safely."

Playing it Smart: What to Do When You're on Your Own, Barron's Educational Series.

Safe at School, Awareness and Action for Parents and Kids Grades K–12, Carol Silverman Saunders, Free Spirit Publishing, 1-800-735-7323.

76 Ways to Protect Your Child from Crime, J.L. Simmons, Ph.D. and George McCall, Henry Holt 1996.

How to Raise a Street Smart Child, Grace Hechinger, HBO Home Video.

Bicycle Safety, video for 5–9 year olds from The American Academy of Pediatrics, 1-800-433-9016.

"Child Alone," a pamphlet on home-alone care and safety issues to and from school, The National Safety Council, 1-800-621-7619, free.

Home Alone: A Kid's Guide can be checked out free from Blockbuster Video or purchased, 1-800-786-8777.

Let's Talk About Living in a World With Violence, an activity book for elementary-age children, James Garbarino, Ph.D., Erickson Institute, 1-312-755-2244. 11.

The National Crime Prevention Council, Municipal & Youth Initiative Unit, 1700 K Street, N.W., Second Floor, Washington, D.C. 20006, 1-202-466-6272.

10

■ ■ ■

Resources for Parents

HELPFUL WEBSITES AND E-MAIL ADDRESSES

Many of these sites are a link to other sources of information and are a resource for parents who want to connect and share ideas directly with other parents across the country. Many local libraries provide Internet access. If you need access to the Internet, check the public library in your area.

www.pta.org Website of the National PTA info@pta.org (E-mail address)
www.futureofchildren.org/ Articles on special education, outcomes of early childhood programs, and other topics of interest
www.parentsplace.com/readroom/spn/index.html Information on how to be a better single parent
www.4j.lane.edu/InternetResources/safety/safety.html Information on both the benefits and dangers of the Internet, what parents can do, guidelines, and rules

177

www.parentsoup.com   A wide range of helpful topics for parents with connections to other sites

www.familyeducation.com   Information about education where parents can share ideas and opinions with other parents on a wide range of educational topics

www.parentsplace.com   Another place for parents to share ideas and offer solutions to problems

www.kidslist@kidscampaigns.org   An electronic backfence discussion group for parents, volunteers, community groups, child advocacy groups

www.communityconnections@lists.servenet.org   A discussion/ newsgroup for community volunteer opportunities and resources

www.org/hot/summit/smart/html   President Clinton's Education Summit website

www.familypc.com   A magazine with advice, articles, and recommendations for families with computers

www.nationalgeograhic.com   *National Geographic* magazine

www.pathfinder.com   *Sports Illustrated for Kids* Contests, information on favorite athletes

www.childrenspartnership.org   frontdoor@childrenspartnership.org (E-mail address) Educates policymakers and parents about technology issues affecting children and works to ensure that technology and quality content are available to all

www.app.org   American Academy of Pediatrics has information on infectious diseases and other childhood ailments

www.epa.org   Environmental Protection Agency website gives information on a new test for radon in school districts

EDUCATIONAL WEBSITES AND BROWSERS FOR KIDS

www.yahooligans.com   A child-safe browser with lots of kids stuff, chat rooms, homework help, etc.

www.netscape.com   Netscape's homepage; lots of search engines and links to other resources

www.microsoft.com/ie   Microsoft Internet Explorer, another web browser, can be downloaded here; comes with built in RSACi filtering, allowing parents to block access to sites with sexual or violent content

www.bonus.com   Website with contests, games, and educational activities

www.nick.com   Website for Nickelodeon, loaded with games and contests

www.animal.discovery.com   Worldwide animal expeditions

www.thomasthetankengine.com   Thomas the Tank Engine

www.americangirl.com   The American Girl site creates a community in which young girls can offer advice to each other in addition to keeping up with the dolls

www.place.scholastic.com/indes/htm   Activities, news, and contests about favorite Scholastic books

www.cyberkids.com   Site for kids' comments in a worldwide community, promoting peace and creativity

www.xplore.com   Links to many other kid sites

www.pbs.org/kids   Favorite shows from PBS

www.4kids.com   Fun activities for children

www.nyelabs.com   Bill Nye the Science Guy site

www.lego.com   Contests and Lego information

quest.arc.nasa.gov   Information on NASA mission to Mars, experiments in space, and communication with astronauts

www.zstarr.com/iho   For older children interested in fossils and the origins of mankind

www.hp-at-home.com/bookclub   Hewlett-Packard's new digital bookclub; an interactive site for ages eight to eighteen to capitalize on their interest in the Internet to encourage reading and writing

www.panasonic.com/panlab   Panasonic Learning Lab, a high-tech environment where kids try the interactive digital technologies

www.fi.ecu   Franklin Institute introduces girls and boys to the world of science; there are two special programs to get girls excited about science: The National Science Partnership and Girls at the Center

www.dinosaur.org   Definitive dinosaur fun site; changes constantly

ORGANIZATIONS THAT CAN PROVIDE RESOURCES TO PARENTS AND KIDS

Family Involvement Partnership for Learning,   800-USA-LEARN, sponsored by the U.S. Department of Education. Has a membership of over 200 organizations who provide information on mentoring programs such as One-on-One, which supports families and children through mentoring and tutoring; and Read°Write°Now! which encourages teens and adults to spend thirty minutes a day reading and writing with a younger child.

Homework Hotlines From Advanced Voice Technologies, 615-885-4170 Offers information to other school systems on setting up their own phone lines. First Tennessee Bank offers support for any school (public, private, or parochial) in its service area to set up Lesson Line; call Leslie Lee at 901-523-4291 to learn more about starting a program out of state, or if you're in state, call the nearest branch of First Tennessee Bank

Minorities in Mathematics, Sciences and Engineering, 513-556-4018 Sponsors in-school and after-school enrichment and career awareness programs for Midwestern students

National Black Child Development Institute,   202-387-1281

The National Wildlife Federation,   800-432-6564 Activities, reading materials, and videos for elementary and middle-school students

The American Federation of Teachers Learning Line,   800-242-5465   Provides educational activities that students can do alone or with friends and family

National Association for the Education of Young Children, 800-424-2460 Publishes a number of books and brochures

Title 1 Schoolwide Project Network, 1904 Association Drive, Reston, Va 22091-1537, 703-860-0200, ext 273; Fax 703-476-5432

National Parent Network on Disabilities, 703-684-6763

The Clearinghouse on Disability Information, 202-205-8241

Federation for Children With Special Needs, 800-331-0688 (in MA only) or 617-482-2915

Hand in Hand, 202-338-7227 Project of the Institute for Educational Leadership and the Mattel Foundation; information available for parents, schools, and communities united for kids; 1010 Wisconsin Avenue, NW, Suite 800, Washington, D.C. 20007; Hand_InHand@goalline.org

Girls, Inc. (was Girls Clubs of America) 212-689-3700 Offers a variety of afterschool programs from encouraging girls in math and science activities to pregnancy prevention

Boys Clubs of America, 404-815-5700 Emphasize career exploration, educational enrichment, health and fitness, drug prevention, and leadership development; 1230 West Peachtree Street, N.W., Atlanta, Georgia 30309

Camp Fire Boys and Girls, 816-756-1950 Helps youngsters seven and older realize their potential through decision making, planning, and problem solving

Junior Achievement, 800-THE-NEW-JA A K–12 program in economic education that partners schools with businesses

Boy Scouts of America, 800-392-2677

Girl Scouts of the USA, 800-223-0624

4-H, 301-961-2800 Offers practical training in nutrition, food production, environmental education, science, and technology; not just for kids in rural areas

Big Brothers and Big Sisters, 215-567-7000 Screens mentors for children, and mentoring is particularly important for children of single parents

The YMCA,   312-977-0031, and The YWCA,   212-614-2700 Can
put parents in touch with after-school programs in their area

The American Camping Association and the National Camp Association Advisory Service,   800-966-CAMP   Free referral
services

The National Assembly of Arts Agencies,   202-347-6352   Information on local arts programs and arts education which has been
added to Goals 2000

Child Care Aware Resource and Referral,   800-424-2246

Child Care Action Campaign,   212-239-0138

Campaign for Kids TV,   310-559-2944 Center for Media and
Values

Center for Media Education,   202-628-2620

National Council on Television Violence,   810-489-3177 33290 W.
14 Mile Rd, Suite 498, West Bloomfield, MI 48331

National Council for Families and Television,   213-876-5959 3801
Barham Blvd, Suite 300, Los Angeles, CA 90068

Yale University Family Television Research and Consultation
Center, 203-432-4565

The Association for Childhood Education International,
800-423-3563   Information and a position paper on constructive
assessment in elementary school, 11501 Georgia Avenue, Suite
315, Wheaton, MD 20902-1924

RECENT PUBLICATIONS FOR PARENTS

From the Harvard Family Research Project:

"Raising Our Future: Families, Schools, and Communities Joining
Together," by Heather Weiss et al., 1995, published by Harvard
Family Research Project, 38 Concord Avenue, Dept A,
Cambridge, Mass. 02138; 617-496-4303. An overview of
seventy-three innovative family support and education programs
around the country in which schools have worked directly with

families and a wide range of community agencies to foster child development.

"Preparing Teachers to Involve Parents: A National Survey of Teacher Education Programs," by Angela Shartrand, Holly Kreider, Marji Erickson-Warfield, 1994. Also available from Harvard Family Research Project (see above). This working paper documents a new trend in teacher education: training teachers to work more closely with families. The paper highlights the key elements of the best practices guiding teachers toward this crucial "new" partnership.

"New Skills for New Schools," Angela Shartrand and Holly Kreider. This report offers a framework for thinking about the content of preservice education for teachers. It also discusses model teacher education programs that are preparing teachers for increased home and community involvement, 1996.

From the National Community Education Publication Series, Larry Decker, managing editor. To order any of these publications, contact the NCEA, 3929 Old Lee Highway, Suite 91-A Fairfax, Virginia 22030, 703-359-8973.

Publications of interest to parents and schools. Titles include: "Teachers Manual for Parent and Community Involvement"; "School Community Centers: Guidelines for Interagency Planners"; "Home-School-Community Relations Manual"; "Rebuilding the Partnership for Public Education"; "Grantseeking: How to Find a Funder and Write a Winning Proposal."

Available from The National PTA Catalog of Resources on Parent/Family Involvement:

"Helping Your Student Get the Most Out of Homework" (also available in Spanish).

"In Someone Else's Shoes: A Guide to Inclusiveness" (includes a video).

"Making Parent-Teacher Conferences Work for Your Student"
(also available in Spanish)
"Rural Parent Involvement"
"Partners in Education" series:
"Teachers and the PTA"
"The Principal and the PTA"
"The School Board and the PTA"
"The Superintendent and the PTA"
"The Busy Parent's Guide to Involvement in Education"
"A Leader's Guide to Parent and Family Involvement"
"The Heart of the PTA: Parent and Family Involvement—A
Manual for Leadership"
"The PTA Parenting Guide"

For Information on ordering these resources, send $1 to National
PTA., 135 S. LaSalle, Dept. 1860. Chicago, Ill. 60674-1860 to receive
a catalog. Or check the above website: www.pta.org

OTHER READING

An excellent book on the subject of helping your child get the most
out of elementary school is called *The Elementary School Handbook*,
by Joanne Oppenheim. It's a parent guide for those with children in
grades K–6 and is published by Pantheon Books, New York, 1989.
The book gives advice on what level of learning is expected for your
child in each grade and how you as a parent can work with the
teacher effectively.

The Read-Aloud Handbook: A Guide for Parents, by Jim Trelease,
is another excellent book. It includes a bibliography of books to read
aloud to children of all ages and includes advice about children and
TV.

The core knowledge series of books by Ed Hirsch, *What Your 1st
Grader Needs to Know*, is published by Dell Publishing, New York,
1993. There is a book for each grade through elementary and middle

school. These highly recommended books cover a wide range of topics and are for parents and children to use together.

The parent's reference book that is the most complete source of information on *all* topics relating to parenting is *The Parents' Resource Almanac,* by Beth DeFrancis, 1994, published by Bob Adams, Inc., Holbrook, Massachusetts. This book provides names, addresses, resources, advice, charts, and book reviews organized by topic of interest.

AFTERWORD

This book has been written as a guide for parents and principals to improve the education of our children. Parents have the power to make our schools work. In closing, I would like to include a favorite quote from Robert F. Kennedy:

> Each time a man stands up for an ideal, or acts to improve the lot of others, or strikes out against injustice, he sends forth a tiny ripple of hope. And crossing each other from a million different centers of energy and daring, those ripples build a current which can sweep down the mightiest walls of oppression.

If you would like to share some ideas from your schools for future editions of this book, the author's E-mail address is kaufmnsl@sprynet.com, or snail mail Susan Mansell in care of the publisher.

INDEX